A CENTURY OF SERBIAN TERROR

1918 - 2018

*In memory of brother Miro, Staff Sergeant of the Croatian Army
(Zagreb, 1969 – Osijek, 2017)*

Nenad Piskač

Title: A CENTURY OF SERBIAN TERROR 1918-2018

Author: Nenad Piskač

Title of the Croatian edition: Stoljeće srbijanskoga terora 1918. - 2018.

ISBN 978-953-48343-0-5

CIP entry available in computer catalogue NSK in Zagreb No. 001013131

Translation: Anica Markov

Proofreading: Marina Škrobica

Front cover: Max Križanić

Graphic design: Graforad (Tomislav Burec)

ISBN 978-1-71680-773-2

Nenad Piskač

A CENTURY OF SERBIAN TERROR
1918 - 2018

Jakovlje, July 2020

CONTENTS

Preface

Most European and some non-European countries devoted 2018 to the memory of the Great War as unprecedented suffering in warfare. The Croatian people have good reason to mark the end of the Great War, later named First World War, because around one hundred and fifty thousand of them died in the various battlefields across Europe (in Galicia, on the Eastern front, in the battles for Soča, in the Dolomites, in Serbia). Given the fact that at the end of the Great War they found themselves on the losing side, practically no attention was devoted to the victims in their ranks. Neglected and forgotten graves and cemeteries of Croatian soldiers of the First World War are today still found in many places despite the fact that on 11 November the Croatian President was invited to mark the end of the First World War in France. Unlike most other nations that participated in the Great War and thereby won their freedom, the Croatian people unfortunately had good reason to suppress the day that marks the end of the Great War in their collective memory, because it did not bring them freedom. After the short-lived State of Slovenes, Croats and Serbs (proclaimed on 29 October 1918), most of the Croatian politicians at the time became frightened of their own autonomy and hastened to bestow the Croatian lands to the Kingdom of Serbia, and urged by Svetozar Pribićević, many of them rushed to Belgrade "like geese into the fog" as Stjepan Radić had warned them. That is how a hundred years ago, on 1 December 1918, after the speech by Ante Pavelić Sr. (dentist), the unification was declared between the South Slav regions that belonged to the Austro-Hungarian Monarchy, and the Kingdom of Serbia.

While the booty of the Great War was still being shared out by the winners in Versailles, the Croats had entered a provisional constitutional and legal administration known as the Kingdom of Serbs, Croats and Slovenes. Despite enthusiastic odes by some Croatian poets, already at the first session of its first government in December 1918, which decided on the equality of the Cyrillic and Latin alphabets in the entire territory of that state, thereby actually starting the imposition of the Cyrillic alphabet on all non-Serbian nations, it became evident what this new state would turn out to be. At the end of 1920, when the leading Serbian politician and king's confidant Nikola Pašić returned from Versailles, a full re-shaping of the new state was undertaken, which named it the Kingdom of Serbs, Croats and Slovenes (*Kraljevina Srba, Hrvata i Slovenaca* - SHS) as declared by the constitution of 28 June 1921. The state was populated by one unidentified people made up of three tribes (Serbs, Croats and Slovenes), while a Serbian-Croatian-Slovene language was declared official. Violence, terror and fraud soon overtook the state and lasted until its end. That is why the author of this book speaks of a century of Serbian terror in Croatia, which is in a specific way easily recognized also in the unitarist language and spelling policy carried out in that state.

The reader will easily notice not only the author's interest in this issue, but also his intention to demonstrate the continuity of unitarist and violent politics until the end of the 1990's, that is, during the period of Socialist Yugoslavia. Some of the features of that belated imperial politics are observed and analysed by the author also in his recent comments on the Croatian Cultural Council web page (hkv.hr).

The author's work is facilitated by some very recent statements made by current Serb politicians, such as the recent fabrication that today a Croatian flag is flying in Knin, which it never did before, or the claim that political relations in south-eastern Europe are complicated by the increasing fragmentation of the Serbian language into a string of political-national varieties.

As an experienced publicist and careful observer, the author is equally keen in his critical judgment and evaluation of recycled nineteenth century views on Greater Serbia (*Načertanije*; "All are Serbs and Serbs are everywhere"), as of aforementioned modern views, where he sees ideas of a Greater Serbia that will undoubtedly draw the interested reader's attention.

Academician Marko Samardžija

Zaprešić, 18 November 2018

A century of Serbian terror 1918 - 2018

A Century of Serbian Terror in Croatia

During the past hundred years, Serbian terror over the Croatian people has been conducted physically and judicially, linguistically and territorially, by myths and propaganda. It continued to liquidate and arrest numerous Croats, it imposed a non-existent language and Cyrillic script in Croatia, it seized Croatian national and historical territories, and it installed myths of Greater Serbia and Yugoslavia into Croatian society and the international community. Serbia holds the same political standpoints towards Croatia in 2018 as it did in 1918.

A historical cross-section from Karađorđević and Pribićević to Vučić and Pupovac

Introduction

World War One broke out when the Bosnian-Serb Gavrilo Princip killed Austro-Hungarian Crown Prince Franz Ferdinand and his pregnant wife on 28 June 1914 in Sarajevo. The Kingdom of Serbia defined its war goals in the Niš Declaration of 1914 - the unification of Croats and Slovenes of the Austro-Hungarian Monarchy with Serbia and Montenegro. About 130,000 Croats died in that war. During the war, the Yugoslav Committee was founded in Paris and by the Treaty of London, the Triple Entente promised Italy large parts of the Croatian coast, islands and the peninsula of Istria, while Serbia granted Italy the right to occupy part of the eastern Adriatic coast, hoping that it would "annex" the rest of the Croatian Adriatic to Belgrade. The Austro-Hungarian Monarchy disappeared from the political map of Europe.

On 29 October 1918, the Croatian Parliament agreed on the decision to terminate the constitutional and legal connections of the Croatian provinces with the Austro-Hungarian Empire and on declaring Dalmatia, Croatia and Slavonia with Rijeka an independent state, which together with other countries under Austro-Hungarian rule entered the joint State of Slovenes, Croats, and Serbs, which included the areas of Slovenia, Croatia, Bosnia and Herzegovina, and Vojvodina and was headed by the National Council. The Serbs living in the territory of this new SHS[1] state, especially politician Svetozar Pribićević and the Kingdom of Serbia, put pressure on the new state with the aim to annex it to Belgrade. Representatives of the SHS, headed by Ante Pavelić Sr. and Svetozar Pribićević went "like geese into the fog" to Belgrade and on 1 December 1918 attended the unilateral declaration of "annexation" of the SHS state

---

1 SHS - *Država Slovenaca, Hrvata i Srba,* the State of Slovenes, Croats and Serbs

to the Kingdom of Serbia and the naming of this state as the Kingdom of Serbs, Croats, and Slovenes. It became immediately apparent that this was not a matter of unification of the two states, but a classic case of occupation. That was the start of a century of Serbian terror on Croatian people. The "annexation" was carried out for the first two and a half years without a state constitution.

The bloody century consists of several periods. The first period lasts from the Serbian occupation of Croatia on 1 December 1918 to the establishment of the Croatian state on 10 April 1941. The second period is from 1941 until the restoration of Yugoslavia in 1945. Then comes the long period of Yugoslav communist totalitarianism from 1945 until the establishment of the Republic of Croatia with Sovereignty Day on 30 May 1991. The last two periods are particularly interesting: the period of Croatian liberation from Serb and Yugoslav communist terror between 1991 and 2000, and the period of creeping restoration of Yugoslav relations and consent for the Balkan positioning of the Croatian state in the years 2000 to 2018. In all these periods, Serbia pursued the same imperialistic foreign policy towards non-Serbian peoples in the Balkans, considering them her colonies.

During the past hundred years, Serbian terror over the Croatian people was conducted physically and judicially, linguistically and territorially, by way of myths and propaganda. It continued to liquidate and arrest numerous Croats, it imposed a non-existent language and Cyrillic script in Croatia, it seized Croatian national and historical territories, and it installed myths of Greater Serbia and Yugoslavia into Croatian society and the international community. The Serb intellectual, clerical and political elite assume that Croats are not *politicki narod*[2] worthy of their own state. Only Serbs are a political people in the Balkans. Where the Serbs in "Serbian states" are not a political people, they have to become that. Consequently, Serb and pro-Serb regimes in the past hundred years

---

2 *politički narod* – literally, a political people - a nation, a political entity or community with comprehesive policymaking powers; in this case, the Croatian people constituted into a nation through their democratically elected independent national state in which ethnic minorities, such as the Serb, can enjoy equal citizenship and other minority rights, but not those connected to the political structure of the state.

endorsed robbery, emigration, sowed fear and committed mass crimes with elements of genocide over the Croats and declared every Croatian State a criminal institution.

Serb terror over non-Serb people has its ideological and political basis in the plan on how to annex neighbouring Slav countries to the Serbian State, created at the time of the fall of the Ottoman Empire in 1844 by the Serbian Foreign Affairs Minister, Ilija Garašanin. The plan was based on the theories of Vuk Stefanović Karadžić – Serbs may belong to three religions and all *štokavci*[3] are Serbs, as well as on the jurisdiction of the Peć Patriarch. The Serb operational premises remain unchanged from Garašanin to the present day: in the Balkans "All are Serbs and Serbs are everywhere". The borders of the Serbian State in the west include all areas where Serbs live and finally, all "Serbian States" have to be "liberated" and "annexed" by any means necessary, as Slobodan Milošević explained at the beginning of 1989: "Institutionally or non-institutionally, constitutionally or unconstitutionally, in the street or indoors, in populist or elitist manner, with or without arguments".

The Kingdom of Serbia sent its agents already in the nineteenth century to areas that it considered "Serbian states" to prepare conditions for the "liberation" of all Serbs and the "annexation" of all "Serbian states". The practice was continued in Croatia this day. During his visit to Croatia in 2018, the Serbian President Aleksandar Vučić presented Milorad Pupovac, member of the Croatian Parliament, as a Belgrade man, and Croatian political elites falsely presented Chetnik Vučić as "European Vučić". A hundred years earlier, Pribićević presented the Serbian King in the same way as the ideal solution for the Croatian issue.

Belgrade always had its people in Zagreb. *Srbobran*, the Zagreb newspaper for the Serb national minority conveyed Belgrade's message by publishing the text by Nikola Stojanović of 1902, in which he negated the existence of Croatian nationality and language. He announced: "The Croats, therefore, are not and cannot be a separate nation, but they are on the path to become Serbian .... No one can stop this process of assimilation." However, the assimilation of Croats into Serbs was stopped

---

3 *Štokavci* – people who speak in the Stokavian dialect (*Štokavina, Štokavica*), one of the three dialects in the Croatian language.

in 1941 and also in 1991 by the establishment of Croatian states. The first one disappeared with the restoration of Yugoslavia, and the second, after the initial success, has been brought to the edge of sustainability by today's "geese in the fog".

On 13 November 1918, the eve of the high treason and occupation, the high representative of the Serbian Supreme Command, Colonel Dušan Simović arrived in Zagreb. He told the representatives of the National Council of the State of Slovenes, Croats and Serbs that Serbia could not allow the formation of a new state on its borders that would include her fellow countrymen within its structure. He added that – according to armament law, Srijem, part of Slavonia, Bosnia and Herzegovina, and Dalmatia belong to Serbia. And he concluded: "Outside of that territory, you can opt at your will." Despite such rhetoric, on 1 December 1918, Croatian political traitors and 'the geese' accepted the politics of turning Croats into Serbs and drowning Croatia within Serbia. This process could not be carried out without coercion, violence and dictatorship. Serbia had, in fact, planned, carried out and maintained the act of "unification" into the Kingdom of SHS exclusively as a means to enlarge Serbia.

1. Period from 1918 to 1941

The Serbian occupation is in direct contradiction of the United States President Woodrow Wilson's fourteen-point plan, according to which the subjugated nations at the end of the First World War have the right to self-determination and independence. The Croatian People's Peasant Party with Stjepan Radić and the Croatian Party of Rights – Frankists, opposed the occupation and unilateral unification. The unconstitutional occupation regime immediately disclosed Greater Serbian intentions and a dictatorial way of holding on to power.

On 4 December 1918, the Chief of Police Grga Anđelinović prohibited the release of the Zagreb daily *Croatia*, due to it announcing the manifesto "to the Croatian people" on the previous day. The manifesto relating to the "unification" read: "Croatian people, they deprived you of your sovereignty and they ceded the sovereign authority over the Croatian people to His Majesty the Serbian King Peter I (…) and no one asked for your decision in that important moment". On 5 December, the

Croats organized massive demonstrations in Zagreb against high treason and the occupation. Anđelinović's gendarmes killed 15 and injured more than 20 demonstrators. Anđelinović was later publicly proud of his "bloody hands". Amongst the December victims, there were 23 non-commissioned officers and officers who were sentenced by the military tribunal to between 18 months and 10 years in prison precisely on 29 December, the day when the Serbian National Assembly confirmed the act of "unification" that was never ratified by the Croatian Parliament. Serbian military colonel Dušan Simović and his officers took over military power in Croatia. In December, the weapons were seized from the Croatian Home Guards regiments, which were partly dissolved and partly merged with the Serbian Army. Croatia was disarmed! The Greater Serbian vampire ball could begin undisturbed. And begin it did!

To start with, Croatia was thoroughly looted. The regime determined - 4 crowns were worth 1 Serbian Dinar. Croats lost three-quarters of their capital in that currency exchange. Croatia lost one billion and 400 million dinars in cash. It also faced the invasion of a corrupt state administration whose roots have not been eradicated to this day. Rudolf Bićanić wrote: "One bloated, slow, lazy, indifferent, desperately formal, inefficient, impractical, irrational and ignorant, but terribly expensive bureaucratic machine based on oriental traditions, methods and moral values that can run only on bribery, which is sustained only by personal favoritisms, or suffers personal political party revenge, and a machine which at the same time holds in its hands complete authority and power in the state ... – is the most suitable setting for corruption, which spreads from there all over the country".

Plunder took place also in the form of heavy burden on imports and exports – paid by the western regions as the biggest importers and exporters, as well as through tax inequality, the state debts that once again Croats mainly paid through taxes. Land and property taxes were up to 4 times higher in Croatia than in Serbia. Railroads were not being built in Croatia, unlike in Serbia, and there were no investments in sea ports, so that Croatia would become increasingly underdeveloped. In 1934, investments in construction facilities in Serbia amounted to 220 million dinars, compared to 38 million dinars in Croatia at the same time. Belgrade raised a hundred-million-dollar loan with 40-year repayment plan on an interest rate of 8 percent for the so-called "Adriatic Railway", which was to connect Belgrade with Kotor over Loznica, Višegrad, Foča, and Nikšić. Croatian personnel held only 15 percent of civil service positions in Belgrade.

At its first meeting on 21 December 1918, the government of the Kingdom of SHS declared "equal use of Latin and Cyrillic alphabet on the whole state territory." That paved the way for the imposition of the Cyrillic alphabet and repression of the Latin alphabet in Croatia, Bačka and Bosnia and Herzegovina - a hundred years on and Croatia still has no law about the Croatian language. The Cyrillic alphabet became an instrument of Serbian hegemony. "Cyrillisation" became rampant after the adoption of the Vidovdan Constitution, especially after the Regulation on Regional Partition. In 33 state regions it became the only script used in state administration, in printed matter, in schools, on banknotes, the military, the railway ... It remained an integral part of official state and language policy for twenty years. A century later, we are witnessing attempts at the "Cyrillisation" of Vukovar and the persecution of its opponents.

The regime of the Kingdom of SHS was also known for changing toponyms. Karlsdorf was renamed "Karađorđevo", Alajbegovci "Peter's Village", Marija Zvijezda "Traveller's Hill". Sutivan became "St. John", Sućuraj – "St. George", Nerežišća - Nerezi. Mali Ker and Stari Ker were renamed after the living Serbian politicians – Pribićevićevo and Pašićevo. There were also frequent changes of surnames to make them "politically correct". Thus, Deutch was changed to Dragić, Dragojević to Prodanović, Franjić to Gjurković, Grünwald to Gorjan, Hajduk to Hajduković, and Spannbauer to Ferić...

Nikola Pašić's occupying government implemented the Orthodox clerical policy from the start. The state budget paid Serbian Orthodox bishops a salary of 10,000 dinars, while the Catholic bishops' salaries were 3,976 dinars. An Orthodox bishop's pension amounted to 9,000 dinars, more than the salaries of two Catholic bishops. The SHS regime confiscated the properties of the Catholic Church through agrarian reform, but as they were not officially transferred in the Land Registry books, the Catholic Church continued paying taxes for its confiscated properties. Catholic hospitals and high schools were in constant danger of being abolished, and priests were imprisoned and killed. The regime and the

Serbian Orthodox Church prevented a concordat arrangement regarding the position of the Catholic Church.

The Election Law stipulated that constituencies could not have less than 30,000 or more than 45,000 inhabitants, which opened the door to electoral manipulations. A greater number of people's representatives were elected in Serbia due to constituencies with a smaller number of inhabitants than those in Croatia.

On 3 February 1919, Radić's party sent a memorandum to the Peace Conference in Paris requesting the right of Croatian self-determination backed by the signatures of two hundred thousand Croats. On 25 March 1919, the Minister of the Interior Pribićević arrested Radić and held him in prison for 11 months. In September 1919, Italy occupied the city of Rijeka by implementing the 1915 Treaty of London, which had the approval of the Serbian government, and now also the Government of the Kingdom of SHS. Italian authorities also abolished Croatian schools in Istria in 1923. Croatia was simultaneously terrorized by Italy and Serbia.

In 1920, in Rapallo in Italy, the Kingdom of SHS officially ceded to Italy the regions of Istria, Cres, Lošinj, Zadar, Lastovo, and Palagruža. It adopted, without the Croats, the so-called Vidovdan Constitution of 1921, which promoted unitarism and state centralism. The Croatian historical wholes were broken down. The institutions of the Croatian Assembly and the Civil Governor's Honour were abolished. Then the State Protection Law was also adopted. This law legalized brutal punishments, even death sentences for those who opposed the "annexation of all Serbian states" occupation policy.

The occupying government ceded Pečuh, Mohač, Barč, Siget and Baja to Hungary, whereby the local Croatian population of 350,000 Croats was divided into Hungarian and Serbian parts. The Serbian regime encouraged the plan of Serbianisation especially of Vojvodina, by settling in Serbian volunteers, the so-called *solunci*[4], and imposing the Serbian language and

---

4 *Solunci* – soldiers in the Serb army who fought in the Balkan wars (all the way to Thessaloniki), and whose heirs even today receive soldier pensions; *solunci* (Serbs) were later moved to the areas of Bačka, Banat, Srijem and Slavonia in order to make up the Serb majority where it did not exist before, alongside the planned exile of Croats, Germans ...

A century of Serbian terror 1918 - 2018

script. In 1922, with the Regulation on the Administrative Division of the State, Croatia was divided into 6 regions. Boka Kotorska was separated from Dalmatia and Baranja was annexed to the Bačka region. In 1924, based on the Roman Treaties between Fascist Mussolini and Pašić, the occupying government ceded the Croatian city of Rijeka to Italy.

As of 28 April 1919, the territory of "hostile regions" that were "annexed" by the state of SHS, becomes subject to Article 298 of the Serbian "Criminal" Code: "Inhabitants of hostile regions occupied by the military will be tried by military courts." Punishment through beatings was introduced by Serbian Colonel Teslić and was approved by Svetozar Pribićević countless times. An advocate of the Republic was punished with 25 blows. The family of a Croat that was shot had to pay for the bullets with which he was killed! More than 30,000 Croats were personally terrorized in the first years of the Kingdom of SHS.

Canadian General F.E. Burham reported upon his return from the Kingdom of SHS: "What is now called Yugoslavia is a bloody pandemonium of shocking horrors, persecutions, plundering, political subjugation and the most terrible reprisals. Citizens of Montenegro, Albanians, Macedonians, Croats and Muslims all share deep hatred against their oppressors, who use the most brutal methods, as in the Middle Ages".

The Serbian regime supported the so-called "non-governmental organizations" of the time, Pribićević's fascist Organisation of Yugoslav Nationalists and Pašić's Serbian National Youth. These terrorist organizations freely exercised terror on persons whose views differed to those of the regime and on those who opposed the Serbian occupation.

The culmination of Serbian terror occurred in 1928 inside the National Assembly in Belgrade, when Serbian representative Puniša Račić shot to death the HSS Party[5] representatives Đuro Basariček and Pavle Tadić, injured Ivan Pernar, Ivan Granđa and Stjepan Radić, the leading Croatian politician, who soon died of his wounds. To any sane mind, any form of Yugoslav community also died in that moment.

---

5 *HSS – Hrvatska seljačka stranka,* Croatian Peasant Party founded 22.12.1904 by brothers Antun and Stjepan Radić, on the doctrine of morality, religion, peace and honesty, the fight for freedom, justice and progress.

In order to calm the dissatisfaction, King Aleksandar Karađorđević proposed to Pribićević the Greater Serbia Amputation Plan, that is, the separation of Croatia from the Kingdom along the line Virovitica-Karlovac-Karlobag, therefore removing Slavonia, Dalmatia and part of central Croatia bordering with Greater Serbia from its territory. The HSS Party rejected the plan. In Zagreb, university professors announced a general strike, which ended up in new bloodshed. The Grand Mayor was removed and the administration was entrusted to Serbian Colonel Maksimović.

In 1929, the King carried out a coup and introduced the so-called January Sixth Dictatorship, under the motto "one king, one nation, one state". The Assembly was dissolved. The Constitution was suspended. National parties and political freedom were prohibited. The Commander of the Royal Guard, Serbian General Petar Živković, known as Pera Kapija, becomes the Head of the Government. The Court for the Protection of the State in Belgrade condemns to death the signatories of the joint Declaration of Croats and Macedonians and their stance for human and national rights, political freedom and full independence for Croatia and Macedonia. Among the convicted is Ante Pavelić Jr., who goes into emigration. Writer Mile Budak takes over the Croatian Party of Rights.

The Kingdom of SHS was renamed the Kingdom of Yugoslavia in 1929 and divided into 9 Banovina [provinces] whose borders did not respect ethnic and geographic units. Croatia was split into 4 Banovina in order to annul the national and historical identity of the Croatian people. Srijem was excluded from Croatia and the Dubrovnik region south of Neretva was excluded from Dalmatia. The policy was implemented under the unitarist slogan "We have created Yugoslavia, let's create Yugoslavs". Yugoslavism becomes the state ideology and brutal force is used to erase national identities.

Such situation causes Croatian reactions. The Ustasha organization - Croatian Liberation Movement - operates in Italy in 1930. At the same time, the HSS Party sends a Memorandum to the League of Nations, in which they emphasize the absolutistic regime of the King and the worsening of the Croatian position and of its people's rights. It warns about the ban on cultural and scientific organizations, the disappearance of the Croatian language from schools and public services, the counterfeiting and erasing of Croatian history in textbooks and that Serbian dictatorship is stopping Croatian cultural progress, neglecting the Catholic faith and damaging tombstones…

The Belgrade regime, however, continues to implement arbitrariness and dictatorship. In 1931, they kill Milan Šufflay, historian, writer, and member of the Croatia Party of Rights. Albert Einstein and Heinrich Mann react in the New York Times demanding that the League of Nations stands up for Croats and gathers "all possible help to protect that small, peaceful and very civilized nation". One year later, an assassination attempt is made in Zagreb on Croatian politician Mile Budak. Later, an attempt is also made on Ivo Pilar, follower of the Party of Rights, geopolitician, who in 1933 published in Berlin the debate "Serbia all over again: Yugoslavia's fateful moment", which is immediately banned.

In 1931, the King imposes a Constitution, once again centralist and in the spirit of Yugoslav unitarism and disguised Greater Serbianism. All "tribal, religious and provincial parties", that is, national parties are forbidden and voting in the elections is public.

In 1932 the publication begins in Italy of the newspaper *Ustasha* - the Croatian revolutionaries' herald. The Ustasha Movement is a reaction to Serbian terror in Croatian lands. Its goal was to establish an independent Croatian state. Demonstrations against Serbian dictatorship take place all over Croatia, in Senj, Ludberg, Kosinje, Split… In 1932, the Ustasha organise the Velebit Uprising[6]. In order to gain approval, the communists also verbally supported the Movement: "The Communist Party addressed the whole Croatian nation inviting them to fully support the Ustasha struggle … Down with Greater Serbia military fascist dictatorship! Yes, to an Independent Croatia!". That same year, the Croats react to the Zagreb

---

6 *Velebitski Ustanak* - the Velebit Uprising, a small-scale attack on the gendarmerie station near Gospić without significant military or strategic consequence, albeit with great repercussions by the authorities, but neverthelss achieving its political goal, particularly abroad, as the first Croatian attempt to be rid of the Serb rule and tyranny.

Points[7], condemning the King's absolutism and Serbian hegemony. They seek the remodeling of the Kingdom of Yugoslavia by returning "to 1918 as the starting point". In response to the Points, the regime immediately arrests Vladko Maček and sentences him to 3 years of maximum-security imprisonment.

From the early twenties, the establishment of numerous Chetnik organizations begins in the territories of the "hostile annexed regions" under the motto "for King and Homeland". Chetniks are in the service of the regime, they support dictatorship, Serbian imperialism, and they serve as a means of Serbianisation and implementation of policies and preservation of the Greater Serbian regime. When King Aleksandar was killed in Marseilles in 1934, Chetnik organizations gained new impetus. Fourty Chetnik subcommittees were established in western Slavonia, which provoked, threatened, attacked and killed political opponents, mostly Croats. In 1935, fifteen Chetnik committees were established in Lika with fifty subcommittees. Between 1933 and 1935, 20 "Chetnik Associations for Freedom and Homeland Honour" were established in the Našice district, 5 in Valpovo and 4 in Donji Miholjac. The most famous Chetnik dukes were Ilija Trifunović Birčanin and Kosta Pečanac, while today they are the war criminals Vojislav Šešelj and Tomislav Nikolić, former President of the Republic of Serbia. Current President Aleksandar Vučić is also a Chetnik. Despite the fact that the Chetniks participated in the aggression against the Republic of Croatia at the end of the twentieth century, their organisations are not officially banned in Croatia, neither is the undemocratic ideology of a Greater Serbia.

The Yugo-regime's repression manifested itself on 19 and 20 February 1935. An unjustified crime known as the Sibinj Victims took place against the peasants of Jakačina Mala, Grizić, Gornji Andrijevci, Donja Vrba and Ruščica - with five killed and many wounded. The peasants' sins amounted to cheering for Maček, exclaiming "long live Croatia!" and "down with the Chetniks!" The brutal response was

---

7 *Zagrebačke punktacije* - Zagreb Points was the name of a resolution released on 7 November 1932 by the Peasant-Democrat coalition and the Party of Rights, but other parties soon produced other Points such as the Novi Sad Points, the Sarajevo Points, the Ljubljana Points, all voicing their demands for the dictatorship to end.

                    A century of Serbian terror 1918 - 2018

intended to frighten the peasantry who favoured the HSS, the leading political force of the Croatian people. In May 1935, Archbishop Antun Bauer handed a memorandum to the King, in which he stood up against the persecution of the Croatian people. Due to merciless dictatorship and continued terror over the Croats, the Croatian Peasant Party founded in 1935 the Croatian Civil Defense, the Croatian Peasant Defense and the *Gospodarska sloga* [an organization aimed at improving the living conditions of the peasantry].

Serbian terror caused new victims in 1937. Without any reason, the gendarmes fired on vehicles leaving a celebration in Senj carrying Croatian youths from Gospić and Pazarište who waved Croatian flags. They killed seven young men and one girl, aged 20 to 25, while five were injured.

Pressed by internal and external forces, the regime accepted the agreement between Dragiša Cvetković and Vladko Maček, whereby in 1939 Banovina Croatia was founded with some elements of sovereignty, which immediately encouraged Serbs from certain Banovina districts to request "annexation" to the Serbian part of the state, and supported by the Serbian Orthodox Church and Belgrade military circles, they founded the Serbian "Krajina" movement with the aim to prevent the formation of any Croatian state. In 1939, the brochure "Krajina – Serbs in our north-western provinces" was published in Zagreb. The Croatian regions listed in the brochure were occupied by Serbs, who tried to annex them to Serbia in 1991. The "Serbs together" movement was also founded. The Serbs tried to break off certain districts away from Banovina Croatia even before the establishment of the Independent State of Croatia. After 1945, they called this the "Anti-fascist Uprising". The Banovina represented a conceptual deviation from royal centralism. Among other initiatives, the movement for the Croatian literary language was established during its existence.

2. Period from 1941 to 1945

The Kingdom capitulated in 1941. The King escaped abroad. The Independent State of Croatia was established. The Ustasha declared it on 10 April 1941 in Zagreb, but in accord with the aspirations expressed by the Croatian people, it was declared in Bjelovar two days earlier, on

8 April. The reaction of the Yugoslav Army and the Chetniks was brutal. In the area of the town of Bjelovar 27 people were killed by 25 April and in the area of the Bjelovar district 72 Croats were killed, among them 19 women and 17 children. On 12 April, the Chetniks attack Slunj. The remainder of the retreating Yugoslav Army kill dozens of civilians in the vicinity of Mostar, burning houses in Croatian villages. At the same time, the Chetniks carry out massacres in Čapljina and the surrounding areas.

The Chetnik Movement was headed by Colonel Draža Mihailović of the Yugoslav Royal Army. A significant number of Serbs from the NDH[8] joined the Movement. King Petar II Karađorđević called them "to take up arms" with the words "Align yourselves into lines in the villages and cities under the guidance of my bravest and most honourable men ... I shall consider all conscripts who join the enemy as traitors!".

The King's Chetnik Mihailović reported "I will fight for the most sublime ideals that a Serb can have: for the liberation and eternal unification of all Serbian countries. (...) Wherever there are Serbian graves, that is Serbian country". The kind of Greater Serbia that Mihailović dreamed of is visible in his Instructions dated December 1941. There he listed the main objectives of the Chetnik battle: 1. Creating the Greater Yugoslavia and within it the Greater Serbia, ethnically clean and within the borders of pre-war Serbia, Montenegro, Bosnia and Herzegovina, Srijem, - Banat – Bačka; 2. Cleansing the state territory of all national minorities and 3. Creating actual common borders between Serbia and Montenegro, and Serbia and Slovenia by cleansing away Muslims and Croats.

Alongside the Chetniks, the communists also rose up against the State of Croatia. Both groups wanted the reconstruction of Yugoslavia. The Chetniks [wanted] a renewal of the Kingdom oriented toward the West and dominated by Serbs. The communists aligned with the Bolshevik ideology and leant on the USSR. Both wanted to gain power in future Yugoslavia. The main obstacles to both were the Croatian people and the Croatian state.

From April onwards, Chetnik crimes against the civilian population are recorded in the districts of Knin and Sinj, and then in Bagaj, district

---

of Gacko, western Bosnia, Podrinje - Foča, Čajnić, Srebrenica, Višegrad and Goražde where Muslims suffer massively, which will be repeated again in 1995 with the Serbian genocide in Srebrenica. Crimes follow in the vicinity of Prozor, western Herzegovina, Biokovo-Imotski area, the vicinity of Split, Dalmatian Zagora. Between 1941 and 1945, the Chetniks killed about 20,000 Croatian Catholics and Muslims in the territory of today's Republic of Croatia, and about 12,000 in Bosnia and Herzegovina.

Faced by the Yugoslav - Chetnik rebellion, the government of the Independent State of Croatia brings out a Decree on the Defense of the People and the State on 17 April. The Bjelovar massacre of Croats was punished by the Croatian government by executing 176 Serbs from the Bjelovar region. The political opponents of the NDH, the extreme Yugoslav nationalists, Chetniks, gendarmes of the former state and communists are imprisoned in camps. In September 1941, the NDH opened a collection and labour camp in Jasenovac, about which the Greater Serbian and Yugoslav propaganda created a myth after the war, in order to declare the Croats a genocidal people unworthy of an independent state. Scientific research about the number of Jasenovac victims has not been made possible to the present day.

Opposing Belgrade's unitarist linguistic policies, the NDH government banned the Cyrillic alphabet and set up the Croatian State Office for Language. The Kuna was introduced as currency. JAZU was renamed HAZU[9]. In June 1941, Germany and NDH agreed on the border between Croatia and Serbia on the line of the old border between Austro-Hungary and Serbia, as the Croats had demanded earlier in the Zagreb Points.

The Communist Party of Yugoslavia with its 8,000 members - half of whom were 'geese' from Croatia - surprised by the breakdown of the Hitler - Stalin pact, decides to fight the German occupiers, who defeated

---

9 *JAZU (Jugoslavenska akademija znanosti i umjetnosti)* – Jugoslav Academy of Sciences and Arts, founded in 1866 under the patronage of Bishop Josip Juraj Strossmayer; from 1991 re-named as *HAZU – Hrvatska akademija znanosti i umjetnosti* – Croatian Academy of Sciences and Arts

the Yugoslav Royal Army in record time. The KPJ[10] is led by Josip Broz, the agent of the Communist International. He holds ninth place on the list of the biggest killers in history. He is responsible for more than a million and 170,000 victims. In 1942 alone, Tito received more than 20,000 Chetniks into his ranks.

The Croatian state was divided into three zones. The first one was the Italian zone of interest. Serbian representatives in northern Dalmatia, Boško Desnica and others, maintained links with the Chetniks and requested the annexation of Bukovica and Ravni districts into the Italian zone and supported the Italians' intention to annex Dalmatia. Desnica joined the Partisans in 1944 as was common practice towards the end of World War II, whereas some 8,000 Chetniks ended up in Great Britain after the war.

The Chetnik and partisan rebellion against the Independent State of Croatia is carried out through terror, which on 27 July escalates into genocide against the Croats in Bosansko Grahovo and the surrounding villages. In the renewed Yugoslavia, 27 July was celebrated as the anniversary of the "Anti-fascist Uprising of the People of Bosnia and Herzegovina". During August and September, partisan troops composed mainly of Serbs, burned the Croatian village of Boričevac and massacred the Croatian and Muslim inhabitants of Kulen Vakuf. At the end of 1941, about 5,000 Chetniks were active in the territory of the Croatian state and by the end of 1944, they numbered about 20,000.

In August 1941, German authorities appoint the Serbian General Milan Nedić, loyal to the Nazis and an advocate of Greater Serbia, at the head of Serbia. By September 1942, he got rid of 94 percent of the Jews in Serbia. The Nazis acknowledged that Serbia was the first *Judenfrei* country in Europe.

During the Second World War, the Partisan Army operates in Croatia. At the end of 1944, it had about 120,000 fighters. Sixty percent of them were Croats and 28 percent Serbs. However, there were 658 Croats and 633 Serbs in the Croatian Headquarters. The Croatian language was already marginalized at that time. In 1944, Vladimir Nazor, the president of ZAVNOH[11], requested that TANJUGs[12] editorial staff publish their

---

10 *KPJ (Komunistička Partija Jugoslavije)* – The Communist Party of Yugoslavia

A century of Serbian terror 1918 - 2018

bulletins intended for Croatian regions in the Croatian language and emphasized that "you have introduced the language of the Belgrade bazaar in the Bulletin, you impose it despite the fact that you are in the territory of the state of Croatia. While you are here in our territory you have to write in Croatian, and when you go to Serbia, write and speak however you please".

At the beginning of September 1943, the NDH revokes the treaties with Rome and declares the annexation of occupied parts of Dalmatia and the islands, while at the end of September, ZAVNOH announces the decision to annex Istria to Croatia and Yugoslavia. At the beginning of April 1945, the Main National Liberation Committee of Vojvodina decides to annex Vojvodina to Serbia, which was confirmed by AVNOJ[13] in August. During the past hundred years, Croatia was being territorially chopped up in war and in peace. This process persists today with suspicious arbitrations and the absence of solutions to territorial issues with Slovenia, Serbia, Montenegro and Bosnia and Herzegovina.

Tito's units enter Dubrovnik in October 1944 and immediately liquidate the Croatian intelligentsia. On the island of Daksa, 36 prominent Dubrovnik citizens were murdered. The killings are carried out by former Chetniks. That was the first mass crime by Yugoslav communists in Croatia.

At the beginning of 1945, partisan units commit crimes against Croats in Herzegovina. By the end of May, 69 friars of the Franciscan Province in Herzegovina are killed. Tito's units enter Zagreb on 8 May 1945, under the command of Serbian generals. The NDH Army and civilian population, shocked by Chetnik killings and communist liquidations, retreat towards

---

11 *ZAVNOH (Zemaljsko anti-fašističko vijeće narodnog oslobođenja Hrvatske)* - State Anti-fascist Council for the National Liberation of Croatia, founded in 1943

12 *TANJUG (Telegrafska agencija nove Jugoslavije)* – Telegraphic Agency of the New Yugoslavia, founded in 1943 as Yugoslavia's official news agency

13 *AVNOJ (Antifašističko vijeće narodnog oslobođenja Jugoslavije)* – Anti-fascist Council for the National Liberation of Yugosavia, established in 1943 as a political umbrella organisation of Yugoslav resistance to the Axis occupation.

Austria. On 15 May, the British military authorities deliver the disarmed Croatian Army and civilians to Tito's butchers in Bleiburg. The British betrayal marks a new stage of terror over the Croats.

3. Period from 1945 to 1990

In May 1945 began the largest massacre of Croats in their history. The communist regime adopted the "Yugoslav ideology" and replaced the king's dictatorship with the revolution. Any crime was allowed in the name of the renewal and survival of Yugoslavia. Mass post-war crimes by Yugoslav communists and integrated Chetniks were carried out from Bleiburg to the Ways of the Cross, so that Yugoslavia could survive as an expanded Serbia. Milovan Đilas said "The Croatian Army had to be destroyed so that Yugoslavia could live". That is, there is no Yugoslavia as long as a Croatian state exists. The very idea of a Croatian state was being eradicated through revolutionary methods. The Serbs saw both the kingdom and communist Yugoslavia as an expanded Serbia. Their leading politicians and executors of systemic Serbianisation were Milovan Đilas until 1945 and Aleksandar Ranković until 1966. The Serbs' role in communist Croatia was to become a political nation that would maintain the Croats and the idea of statehood in obedience.

Liquidations start of "national enemies" without court sentence and record. More members of the NDH government were murdered than the number of Hitler's top Nazi leaders sentenced to death in Nuremberg. More than 600 Catholic priests were murdered. When the partisans entered Gospić, 28 percent of the inhabitants were killed, in order to ethnically cleanse the route to Karlobag at the tip of Greater Serbia. More Croats were persecuted, tortured or shot in the post-war period than those in all the countries of the Axis forces put together. In the renewed Yugoslavia, Croats were left without half of the territory of the Independent State of Croatia, as well as without Boka Kotorska and a large part of Srijem.

Many mass killing grounds are found today across Slovenia and Croatia. Dubrovnik's destiny in 1945 was also experienced by other cities involved in the final war operations. More people were killed in 1945 than in 1941. There is a popular saying still commonly used today: it was easy to survive the war, but it was difficult to survive the "liberation". After the end of the war mass execution grounds of innocent victims appeared in Dravograd, Kočevski Rog, Maribor, Macelj and Varaždin.

The authorities introduce totalitarianism. They decimate journalists, 38 out of 330 journalists were killed and 131 escaped abroad, while 45 changed their professions and only 27 received their journalist licenses. Zagreb's Archbishop Aloysius Stepinac was sentenced to 16 years in prison, where they were poisoning him. The highly-positioned Croat, communist Andrija Hebrang was arrested and killed in Belgrade because he advocated Croatian interests. A concentration camp was opened in July 1949 for political opponents on the island of Goli Otok. The camp was in operation until 1989, a whole 40 years!

The communist regime soon released data on war losses of 1,700,000 people. The actual population loss was around 1,014,000. Serbian propaganda took advantage of the difference to create the myth that between 700,000 and one million Serbs were killed in Jasenovac during the war. That myth is being spread around even today by politicians of the Serbian national minority in Croatia, and by Serbian foreign politics lobbyists. Dr Franjo Tuđman was the first person to oppose the Jasenovac myth in Yugoslavia.

Croatian emigrants create political organizations with the aim to establish a Croatian state, and the *Croatian Review* is published in Buenos Aires. The Catholic Faculty of Theology is excluded from the structure of study programmes at the University of Zagreb. Yugoslavia breaks off diplomatic relations with the Vatican due to Stepinac' proclamation as Cardinal.

The practice of Serbianising the Croatian language continues. The Novi Sad Agreement of 1954 determines that the literary language of Croats, Serbs and Montenegrins is uniform and the different pronunciations and use of Latin and Cyrillic scripts are of equal standing. That Agreement is annulled in 1967 when Croats adopt the Declaration on the Denomination and Status of the Croatian Literary Language. Tito condemned that Declaration. The authors, signatories and Croatian institutions who initiated the Declaration are exposed to political pressures and excluded from public life.

In the late sixties, the totalitarian regime begins to introduce the term "Croatian nationalism" which was to serve to label and persecute Croats. In 1970 the Serbs in the Communist Party accuse Croatian communists of allowing the spread of nationalism. The following year, Marko Veselica and Šime Đodan are expelled from the Party because of their writings on economic inequality for Croatia within the SFRJ[14]. That same year, 1971, Croatian emigrants in Sweden assassinated the Yugoslav Ambassador. They were sentenced to life imprisonment. Tito gives in to the Serbs and demands decisive action from Croatian communists against the nationalistic and separatist tendencies in Croatia, and attacks the cultural institution *Matica Hrvatska* [Matrix Croatica] and the Student Union. The SKJ[15] criticizes communists from Croatia, Savka Dapčević-Kučar, Pero Pirker and Miko Tripalo, stating that they encouraged nationalism and chauvinism. Croatian universities go on strike in support of Croatian leadership and advocate for political changes and economic equality, in order that the foreign currencies which Croats earn can remain in Croatia. The police react with violence and suppress the "Croatian Spring". The Croatian leadership is removed. The work of *Matica Hrvatska* is forbidden. Many prominent Croats suffer, among them the future Croatian President Dr Franjo Tuđman, then Vlatko Pavletić, Hrvoje Šošić, Dražen Budiša, Vlado Gotovac and others. Between then and the end of the 1980's, the so-called "Croatian Silence" prevails in Croatia.

During that period Croats try again to get out of Yugoslavia. In Canada, they establish the Croatian National Council with the goal to liberate the Croats. In 1976, Croatian emigrants hijack an airplane in America demanding that the world press publish data on the Yugoslav repression over the Croatian people. Zvonko Bušić was convicted to life imprisonment in the United States of America. In 1978 the Yugoslav UDBA[16] murdered Bruno Bušić, Tuđman's collaborator and one of the most politically active emigrants, an advocate of reconciliation between

---

14 *SFRJ (Socialistička Federativna Republika Jugoslavija)* - Socialist Federative Republic of Yugoslavia, 1963-1992.

15 *SKJ (Savez komunista Jugoslavije)* - The League of Communists of Yugoslavia, 1919-1990.

16 *UDBa (Uprava državne bezbednosti)* - State Security Administration, 1946-1990.

A century of Serbian terror 1918 - 2018

the Croatian left and right parties. Between 1945 and 1990, the Yugoslav regime liquidated in the most brutal manner at least 67 Croats outside Croatia. Not only was the renewed Yugoslavia created on crime, it would not have been able to survive without the oppressive mechanism. The trial for the murder of emigrant Stjepan Đureković was held only recently, but in Germany.

The whole repressive, military, diplomatic and managerial mechanism of the Yugo-communist state was thoroughly Serbianised. Serbs moved into Croatian regions under the motto "brotherhood and unity." Mostly as policemen and JNA officers, heads of state administration and public affairs. At the same time, the doors were opened to Croats from Croatia and from Bosnia and Herzegovina for "temporary work abroad". About one million Croats emigrated to the West. This opened-up job positions for Serbs, who then administered the Croatian emigrants' foreign currency funds [sent home to Croatia].

Aggressive agitation and propaganda, single-minded beliefs and Marxist ideology were introduced into the society. The peasants were left without land and were forced to enter working cooperatives formed on the Soviet *kolhoz* and *sovhoz* models. An agreed history came about. It is persuasive about the lies on how, under communist leadership, wild tribes entered into an unbreakable Yugoslav togetherness. Workers are referred to as "self-managers". Companies as "work organisations". The salary - "personal income". Yugoslavia is maintained by western credit and Croatian foreign currency from abroad, and by repression and single-mindedness from within.

When Tito died in 1980 it was clear that Yugoslavia will disintegrate. The Serbs return to Garašanin's plan to create the Greater Serbia, which they modernise in 1985 with the SANU Memorandum[17] emphasizing the false claim that Serbs outside their Socialist Republic are endangered and need to be "liberated" and "annexed" alongside the others' territories. All Serbian political, religious, intellectual, media and military forces are harnessed in order to create a Greater Serbia from crumbling Yugoslavia. In that atmosphere, the Communist Alliance of Yugoslavia in Belgrade

---

17 *SANU Memorandum (Memorandum srpske akademije nauka i umetnosti)* – Srbian Academy of Sciences and Arts Memorandum 1985-1986.

broke up in 1990, and only a thoroughly Serbianised Yugoslav National Army was all that remained of that state. In August of that year, a new Serb riot exploded against the newly established Republic of Croatia, following the same scenario that was implemented against the establishment of the Independent State of Croatia and that of Banovina Croatia. The old Serbian expansion plan toward the West did not envisage any Croatian state.

4. Period from 1990 to 2000

The year of 1990 began with the re-registration of *Matica Hrvatska*, but also with the registration of the Serb Cultural Association *Zora*, with Jovan Opačić as president. In July he declared in the cultured Serbian manner: "Should the Yugoslav Federation disintegrate, then the integral Serbian state will be from Lika and Kordun to Pirot and from Subotica to Dubrovnik."

At the first democratic elections, the battle was fought between the leading political party HDZ[18] with Tuđman as the leader who promotes the Croatian state, then the Socialist Alliance and the Communist Alliance - who advocate remaining within Yugoslavia, and the Coalition of the National Pact, which was a continuation of the Pact of 1971, and which supports a treaty alliance between Croatia and other republics. The communist leader of Yugoslav orientation, Ivica Račan, labels the HDZ "the party of dangerous intentions" since it was the only party that envisaged a free Croatian state. The communist presidency of the Socialist Republic of Croatia evaluates that the first HDZ parliamentary session held in February 1990, was "an attack on democracy". Simultaneously, about 50,000 Serbs and Yugoslavs gathered in Petrova Gora[19] at the beginning of March 1990, cheering the Greater Serbian leader Slobodan Milošević, with the words: "This is Serbia!", "We will kill Tuđman!" and "We do not want divisions!" They sang "Oh, Slobodan, Serbian son, when will you come up to Udbina".

---

18 *HDZ (Hrvatska demokratska zajednica)* – Croatian Democratic Union
19 *Petrova Gora* – a hill range in the central Kordun region along the border with Bosnia and Herzegovina, administratively part of Karlovac county.

A century of Serbian terror 1918 - 2018

Between the two electoral rounds, the Serbianised JNA[20], without actual resistance from the communist government, seizes on its departure the weapons of the Croatian Territorial Defense. For the second time since 1918, Croatia was completely disarmed. Milošević's closest collaborator Borisav Jović wrote "We practically disarmed them. Formally, the Chief of Staff did this, but in fact, it was according to our order. The Slovenes and Croats reacted sharply, but cannot do anything about it". Croatia was deprived also of any legal purchase of defense weapons, due to particular effort by Yugoslav diplomat Budimir Lončar. Ten years later, he was to became advisor to the President of the Republic!

Alongside the disarming, the relationship of the Serbianised JNA and the Yugoslav presidency towards the democratic processes in Croatia is also evident in making it impossible for Croatian police to try to establish peace and security in disrupted rebellious areas with the transfer of Croatian, Slovene and Albanian soldiers and officers from Croatia to territories of other republics, while simultaneously bringing in single-nation (Serbian) military compositions to garrisons in Croatian areas, as well as in arming rebelled Serbs in Croatia. The JNA generals' structure was composed of 70 per cent Serbs and 30 per cent others. Of the total number of active JNA military members, there were 54.43 per cent Serbs and 12.31 per cent Croats. Under such circumstances, the HDZ Party takes over power in Croatia in democratic elections. The first session of the Croatian Assembly was held on 30 May, which the Serbs boycotted because of the stage-managed Mlinar case. For the following ten years, 30 May was celebrated as Statehood Day up until the regressive, Yugo-communist coup in 2000, which was supported from abroad.

Branko Marijanović, the Vice President of the Serbian Democratic Party, expressed the point of view of most Serbs in Croatia in his speech delivered in Smoković on 16 June 1990. He said "We win the elections even after the elections. The elections which we lost during the elections, we win afterwards, because people are now voting between our party and the other parties. Instead of the five-pointed red star, they are now

---

20 *JNA (Jugoslavenska narodna armija)* - The Yugoslav Peoples Army, was the military of Yugoslavia 1945-1992 and primary part of the Yugoslav armed forces.

wearing some dice[21], they are not communists, they are gamblers. You know that we have…frozen relations with the Croatian Assembly and with all parties centered on Croatia, including Račan's SKH SDP[22]…If Croatia is our homeland and Yugoslavia is our homeland and our love, and if Kosovo is our national soul…we are creating our community of municipalities".

Croatia's democratic government continuously tried to establish accord with the Serbs. Despite that, the Greater Serbia propaganda attempted to justify their rebellion and anti-constitutional activity by pointing at the Croatian government's poor relations towards the Serbs. Serbian politicians in Croatia accepted such thesis, which has been repeated countless times until our days, and which was formulated by the key Belgrade man in Croatia: "Individual, group and mass liquidations of Serbs began already in the first half of 1991 (even earlier, according to some). Innocent civilians were taken from their homes, common shelters, from work or from the street, and they ended up killed in rivers and mass graves". In 2013, simulating Serbian peril and Croatian fascism, representative Milorad Pupovac entered the Croatian Parliament wearing a yellow tape with the word "Visitor" written on it.

The unconstitutional activity of redrawing the territorial-administrative structure of Croatia had, however, begun already in June 1990, when the rebels in Knin decided upon the structure of the communities in the municipalities of northern Dalmatia. The Serbs in Donji Lapac, Obrovac, Dvor, Vojnić, Glina, Kostajnica, Gračac and Benkovac also adopted unconstitutional decisions. The Serb rebels declared that "for Serbs in Croatia, all constitutional and legal changes, which negate their sovereignty as a nation and reduce their autonomous right to "secession" and "annexation" to Serbia are null and void". The leaders of Serbian rebels in Croatia and Belgrade claimed that "it is people that secede from Yugoslavia, not states".

---

21 *kocke* - dice, a wrong and malicious reference to the historic Croatian Coat of Arms of white and red squares

22 Ivica Račan, Prime Minister of Croatia 2000-2003 and leader of the *SDP (Socijaldemokratska partija Hrvatske)* – Social Democratic Pary of Croatia, founded 1990. *SKH (Savez komunista Hrvatske* - League of Communists of Croatia, 1937-1990).

A century of Serbian terror 1918 - 2018

After their "community of municipalities", the Serb rebels founded unconstitutional "autonomous regions" in Croatia: "SAO Krajina"[23] (Knin, 21 December 1990), "SAO Western Slavonia" (12 August 1991) and "Serbian Region Slavonia, Baranja and western Srem" (Beli Manastir, 25 September 1991) with the aim to unite the "Serbian regions" with those in Bosnia and Herzegovina, but ultimately with the Serbian state. After the "Serbian autonomous areas" the "Republic of Serbian Krajina" was founded.

The armed rebellion of Serbs in Croatia began on 17 August 1990 with the "declaration of war" and gatherings of armed terrorists in front of police stations in Knin, Benkovac, Obrovac, Gračac, Titova Korenica, Dvor na Uni and Donji Lapac. The roads in the Knin area were blocked. The tourist season was undermined. Somewhat later, 17 August became the "state" holiday in the occupiers' Republic of Serbian Krajina, the day of the uprising of the Serbian people. The same date was adopted by Serbia in its legislation.

When testifying in the Hague about the "spontaneous uprising of the people", Slobodan Lazarević, Serbian military intelligence officer, explains that "President Milošević had delegates in Krajina, who were in charge of fulfilling all his wishes. His representatives were, almost without exception, agents of the Serbian State Security Service - SDB. They were in Krajina from the beginning and the allegedly "spontaneous" 1990 rebellion against the Croatian authorities was organized from Belgrade".

Borisav Jović clarified what was happening at the beginning of the nineties: "an ethnic map of Serbian territory is being prepared, especially for Bosnia and Herzegovina and for Croatia to clearly show the territory where Serbs are in the majority; from Šibenik, across Lika, Bosanska Krajina, by the Sava River to Bijeljina there are mostly Serbs. In the centre of Bosnia, there are Muslims. The Serbs also cross Sandžak by the Drina river, so that Muslims cannot unite. That is the future territory of Serbia".

---

23 *SAO Krajina (Srpska autonomna oblast Krajina)* – self-proclaimed Serb autonomous province within the independent Croatia, which was in 1991 proclaimed *RSK (Republika Srpska Krajina)* - The Republic of Serbian Krajina, but remained internationally unrecognized.

The dismantling of democratically elected authorities in Croatia was the main objective of the Serbianised Yugoslav Presidency and the highest ranks of the JNA military. For this reason, on 9 January 1991, the Presidency of SFRJ ordered that "all armed compositions which are not within the united SFRJ armed forces or the Internal affairs forces, and whose organisation is not established according to federal regulations, must be dismantled". Croatia had, in fact, started to organise security, anti-terrorist and special police forces.

On 28 February 1991, Douglas Hogg, the second man in the British Foreign Office, comes to Zagreb and offers President Tuđman the old idea advocated since 1918 by the "geese in the fog" and then followed by Tito's communists and the Coalition of the National Agreement in 1971, which the Greater Serbs would gladly accept, namely, that "all republics declare their sovereignty, but then immediately simultaneously also reach agreement about the union of Yugoslav republics, where the basic interest would be the common market and a single voice in the EU". He added that Milošević had told him that "the solution is either the Yugoslav Federation or the Greater Serbia". This British thesis was favoured by Račan's communists, but when it was not accepted after Croatian independence from Yugoslavia, they left the Assembly and mentally remained in Yugoslavia. While Tuđman listened to such pro-Yugoslav ideas and talked with their advocates, he was creating a military force without which there would be no Croatian state.

The JNA counter-intelligence service led by Serbian General Aleksandar Vasiljević carries out diversions all over Croatia, arrests and through sabotage, spreads the sense of insecurity and the need for JNA intervention. The rebel Serb leadership does not accept the legitimate authority's invitations for discourse. Already earlier the former members of the Serbian Democratic Party had left the Parliament and at the end of January 1991, eleven delegates of Serbian nationality, elected on the communist lists of SKH-SDP and Socialist Party announced that they were leaving the Assembly. Namely: Marko Atlagić, Dušan Badža, Milorad Bekić, Stevan Cupać, Petar Džodan, Savan Grabundžija, Ilija Knežević, Branka Kuprešanin, Veljko Pjevac, Milivoj Vojnović and Jovan Vukobrat.

Serbian rebels carry out provocations in Pakrac, Plitvice… and after the intervention by Croatian police, the JNA enters with its armoured units. The first Croatian police officers are killed. The JNA is deployed along the lines planned by the Greater Serbia strategists as the borders of the new Serbian state. In 1991, Vuk Drašković, the influential warmonger and president of the Serbian Renewal Movement, confirms the continuity of the Greater Serbian politics: "The optimal program is (…) the unification of all Serbian regions into one state. One optimal program must also count on, for example, Skadar. (…) If our land is up to Ogulin, and if it is written in the *Načertanje*, then our ideal will be to reach Ogulin in favourable historical circumstances. (…) It is insane and unimaginable to insist now on merging Temišvar to Serbia, but in 1945, had Draža Mihailović won, we could have achieved that".

On 27 June 1991, the leadership of Serbian rebels from Croatia and the Serbian representatives from "Bosanska Krajina" issued the "Declaration on the Unification of the SAO Krajina and the Communities of the Municipality of Bosnian Krajina". The contents of the Declaration show that the ultimate goal of the renewed Greater Serbian politics and Serbian rebellion in Croatia - expressed by the principle that "all Serbs live in one state" – was "the creation of a unified state in which all Serbs in the Balkans will live".

Between 2 May and 2 August 1991, at least 170 Croatian war veterans were killed in the attacks by the JNA and Serbian paramilitary units, among them 83 Croatian policemen. Most Croatian policemen were killed in eastern Slavonia – 45, in Banovina - 23, in Lika - 6, in western Slavonia - 5 and in Dalmatia – 5. The Serbian aggression on Croatia, which was openly carried out since summer 1991, had the objective to split the Croatian territory and then occupy Croatia or at least those parts of Croatian territory which the Greater Serbian leaders wanted to attach to the planned unified Greater Serbian state. Baranja was mostly occupied already in August 1991 by the breakthrough of the Novi Sad corpus of the JNA from Vojvodina (Yugoslavia, Serbia), and the occupation of Slavonia was planned by the coordinated operation of the JNA from Serbia and Bosnia and Herzegovina in autumn 1991. Parts of Slavonia, Dalmatia, Lika, Banovina and Kordun were occupied by the end of 1991. The JNA in 1991 acted in the same way as the Serbian Army of 1918.

In October 1991, French philosopher and politician Alain Finkielkraut described the character of the war against Croatia and the role of the JNA in *LeMonde*: "Croatia is not the battle-field of a civil war, as some persistently repeat, but of a military invasion. The navy, the "migs", tanks and firearms are entirely on one side, on the side of the "federal" army. Regardless of how much ideology remains in it, that army is not federal, it is communist, and it is made up of Serbs. It is not a fight against a re-emergence of the Ustasha fascism, but against the decision made by Croats in a democratic manner to be the masters of their own destiny, not to be subject to a hostile government anymore, and to establish a sovereign state within the European community. This is not an attempt to protect Serbian minorities in Croatia, but rather to punish Croats, treating their memorials as enemy ones, and seizing their territory in favour of Serbia".

Three days later, JNA planes bombarded Banski Dvori with the aim to kill President Tuđman.

In the areas controlled by Serbian forces, nearly all non-Serbian inhabitants were either killed or expelled, even the Serbs who did not support the Greater Serbian politics, and the Croatian cultural and sacral heritage was plundered and destroyed. Nevertheless, Croatia was not defeated in 1991. Of the many Croatian cities that were attacked, the Serb aggressor succeeded to occupy Knin, Petrinja and to destroy Vukovar. In Vukovar, during the Serbian aggression at least 1,739 people were killed, mostly civilians and at least 2,500 were wounded. After the occupation, about 22,000 Vukovarans were expelled, and more than 4,000 people from the Croatian Podunavlje region were forcefully taken to the territory of Serbia. At least 2,796 prisoners were tortured and abused in camps and prisons in Serbia. The youngest prisoner was 15 years old and the oldest was 81. At least 266 persons were taken from the Vukovar hospital, and they were killed in various places of execution. 200 of them were killed on the Ovčara farm, including 20 Vukovar hospital employees. In 1996, 200 corpses aged 16 to 72 were exhumed from a mass grave. Serbian occupiers renamed the Stjepan Radić Street to Puniša Račić Street, after Radić's killer.

Those were the implementation methods of the Memorandum of the Serbian Academy of Sciences and "Arts" and Garašanin's *Načertanije*, which states: "The basis of Serbian politics is to try to attach all neighbouring regions to Serbia and not to limit it to the current borders." The Croatian "geese" and Croatian communists never understood that the Serbian politics is permanent and that any ingratiation to it constitutes - a betrayal of Croatia.

Croatia freed itself from the forces of Greater Serbia by its "own military forces and with God's help" in 1995. Čedo Bulat, the commander of the 21st Kordun Corpus, the so-called "Serbian Krajina Army", signed the surrender to the Croatian Army on 8 August 1995. A great number of Serbs from the liberated areas left together with the Serbian Army. The self-exodus of the Serbs was repeated in 1998, after the peaceful reintegration of Podunavlje. Why did they leave? They left because they did not create the Greater Serbia on Croatian territory. The same year, 1998, despite the exposure to the eight-year long aggression, the Croats won third place in the World Cup Football competition!

The Croatian military achievements against the occupying forces in 1995 led to the Dayton Agreement. Despite establishing peace in Bosnia and Herzegovina, this Agreement was never ratified in Bosnia's Parliament, and the guaranteed right of all refugees and exiles to return to their homes, especially in the region of the "Serbian Republic", in fact remained unfulfilled. The US Information Agency, therefore concluded: "In March 1996 we sent an analysis of the US State Agency to Zagreb, dated December 1995, which illustrates the issues of Croats in Bosnia and Herzegovina that should be used as arguments for the following: 1) Inability for 200,000 Croats to return to the territory controlled by the Army of Bosnia and Herzegovina; 2) specifically the issue of Bugojno; 3) the international community is neglecting the violation of human rights and war rights by the Army of Bosnia and Herzegovina, which hinders the implementation of the Federation (at least eight massacres); 4) the inability for Croats to access Sarajevo media (*de facto* their exclusion from the politics and diplomacy of the Sarajevo Government); 5) close ties between Sarajevo and Tehran".

The American Agency noted that the inability of 200,000 Croats to return to central and northwest Bosnia was of greater importance for the Federation than the Mostar issue, where Muslims represented 2% of the Bosniak population, while the number of above-mentioned expelled

Croats amounted to 25% of the total population in the Federation of Bosnia and Herzegovina. The analysis warned that 42% of Bosnian Croats suffered physical damage and injuries, compared to the 15% by Bosniaks and 13% by Serbs. Despite that, according to the Agency's survey, the Croats proved to be the most disposed to forgive their enemies and support Western democracy.

Let's not forget that in 1918, Bosnia and Herzegovina was "annexed" to the Kingdom of Serbia as an integral part of the SHS state. Under the Dayton Agreement 77 years later, Bosnia and Herzegovina was a divided nation with 2 entities and 3 constitutive nations. Thanks to the aggression, the Serbian entity got 49% of the territory, while 51% went to the Federation of Bosnia and Herzegovina despite the fact that Serbian politics were the main guilty party for the bloodshed in both the monarchy and in communist Yugoslavia.

According to Andrija Hebrang, Minister of Health during the war, 6,891 Croatian soldiers and 7,263 civilians were killed on the Croatian side during the Serbian aggression. About 47% of the civilians killed were older than 60, and 44% were women; 4,285 children were left without one parent, and 54 without both parents. More than 400 children were killed.

In the unoccupied areas 30.578 persons were wounded, out of which as many as 7,169 civilians and 21,959 Croatian war veterans. There were 1,044 children among the wounded civilians. There were 188 children left disabled from the consequences of wounding. Out of the total number of civilian deaths, more than 54% perished in eastern Slavonia, and more than 12% in the area under the administration of the United Nations Forces.

The Serbian aggression on Croatia completely destroyed or damaged a total of 1,313 sacral buildings: 265 parish churches, 306 other churches, 221 chapels, 252 parish houses and halls, 80 monasteries, 62 cemeteries and 127 outdoor crosses.

So far, more than 150 mass graves have been discovered with at least 3,995 victims and about 1,200 individual tombs of the victims of the Serbian aggression. At least 195,000 residential units were either destroyed or damaged in Croatia, and about 120 business centres and 2,423 cultural monuments. During the first year of the Serbian aggression, 590 villages were stricken, and 57 Croatian municipalities, of which 35 were completely destroyed and 34 suffered heavy damages, among them also larger cities. Just the direct war damages were estimated by the Croatian government in 1999 to be US$ 37.1 billion. According to more recent research, the total war damage between 1991 and 2004 amounts to about US$ 142 billion. The direct war damage amounts to US$ 56.5 billion and the indirect damage amounts to US$ 85.5 billion.

According to the 2004 GDP, Croatia lost between 7.5 and 9 years of annual gross communal productivity up to 2015 due to the Serb aggression. The total Croatian cost of the last Serbian aggression must include the damages suffered by the Croats in Bosnia and Herzegovina, which are also huge. In Bosnia and Herzegovina, about 9,900 people died or disappeared from 1992 to the end of 1995. More than 400,000 Croats had to flee their ancestral heritage in the attacks of Serbian forces or the Army of Bosnia and Herzegovina. The estimate is that at least half of the expelled Croats did not return to Bosnia and Herzegovina after the war.

The generally accepted conclusion is: "The organizations that were involved in gathering the facts, such as the United Nations, The U.S. Foreign Office, the CIA, Helsinki Watch and other, have unanimously concluded that the Serbs committed 90 percent of crimes in the Balkan war. Additionally, they concluded that the Serbs committed 100 percent of the genocide according to the definition of genocide given by the UN, that is, organized, planned and systematic destruction of a nation as a whole or partially, based on ethnicity, religion or other group identity".

5. Period from 2000 to 2018

Despite the military and diplomatic victory, President Tuđman was concerned about the state and the nation towards the end of his life. He said "Various scatterbrains and troublemakers, stirrers and brainless wonders, useless dilettantes and simply – sold souls, want to devaluate the magnificent resurrection of Croatian freedom and independence, and the mighty Croatian Storm war victory." For this reason, he incorporated Article 141, named Tuđman's Fortress, into the Constitution, which made legal waddling into new, principally Yugoslav, fogs impossible.

In 2000, the Government was taken over by the crypto-communist coalition of pro-Yugoslav orientation headed by Račan and Mesić. Then Sanader, Kosor and Josipović followed their path. Croatia was also ruled by Milanović's government, the sixth worst in the world, in which a large number of ministries were led by Serbs, even the descendants of the bloody Anđelinović from 1918. Plenković even invented a new type of government - the so-called "inclusive government" which is thoroughly dependent on Vučić's Pupovac.

Over the past 18 years state holidays are changed, the Chamber of Counties is abolished, the Croatian State Assembly renamed Croatian Assembly, the semi-presidential system is abolished, and the Constitution adapted for the partial aims of the elite. A farcical electoral system is established in which not all Croatian citizens are equal. Croatian emigrants are expelled from political life, the minorities are inserted. Croatians in Bosnia and Herzegovina are neglected. The proactive foreign policy is replaced with a passive one. The governments agree to deal with inter-state problems by means of dubious arbitrations instead of international courts. The Serbian element is privileged again. Croatian war veterans are repeatedly betrayed. More than 3,000 Croatian veterans committed suicide. The people and the state are heavily in debt. On top of which Vinkovački Križevci still carries the name – Karadžićevo!

In August 1996 the aggressor acknowledged defeat with the Agreement on Normalization of Relations, which also stipulated a Compensation Agreement regarding payment for all destroyed, damaged or missing property as a preamble to the payment of war compensation. During the past 18 years, no Government has approached the issue of fulfillment of that damage Compensation Agreement. Constitution Article 141 was harshly disrupted several times. The external debt escalated enormously. Emigration is a daily occurrence. The demographic downfall is threatening the extinction of the Croatian nation. A hundred years after its "annexation", Croatia is at the bottom of the European Union's economy, mostly due to the new Balkan positioning of the state and the rehabilitation of Yugoslavism and Chetniks by the political elite.

The Serbian aggression is re-named a civil war. Anti-fascism has become the greatest virtue. In 2018 the SDP representative Nenad Stazić wrote: "It seems that in May 1945 the job was not done thoroughly

   A century of Serbian terror 1918 - 2018

enough. What sloppiness on the winner's part!" Investigations on massive communist and Chetnik post-war crimes are sabotaged. The Yugoslav and Greater Serb myths are still being promoted. Chetniks have become anti-fascists in Serbia and parliamentary delegates in Croatia, such as Minister Vojislav Stanimirović of the occupier Government of the Republic of Srpska Krajina. Croatian geese are renewing monuments of the Chetnik 1941 uprising. A large part of the work of the Yugoslav State Security Administration (UDBa) was taken over by so-called government organizations on a state budget. The policemen who investigate Serbian crimes, such as those on Ovčara, are suspended. The opponents of Cyrillization of Vukovar are arrested and tried. Serb war veterans who defended Croatia are marginalized. Serbia, with Croatian representatives, marks Victory and Homeland Thanksgiving Day as Remembrance Day of Killed and Displaced Serbs.

Dejan Jović, the Serbian intellectual from the British stable, a professor on Croatian salary and Pupovac's associate, considers that the referendum on Croatian independence was "very non-liberal" and that it was not held in free and honest circumstances. Later, in his book he lies that "the myth about the Homeland War" (Croats against Serbian aggression) is a threat to freedom in Croatia, especially for minorities.

Croatia is exposed to the media terror of integral Yugoslavism. A Yugo-feeding chain has been established in which significant roles are played by: Tomislav Jakić, Mirko Galić, Igor Mandić, Jelena Lovrić, Gojko Marinković, Inoslav Bešker, Goran Radman, Drago Hedl, Boris Dežulović, Ante Tomić, Miljenko Jergović, the late Jasna Babić, Slavenka Drakulić, Mirjana Rakić, Saša Leković, Zoran Šprajc, Jurica Pavičić, Aleksandar Stanković, Branimir Pofuk, Boris Pavelić, Drago Pilsel, Mladen Pleše, Branko Mijić, Matija Babić, Ladislav Tomičić, Tomislav Klauški...

The practice of "agreed history" has continued. Historians Hrvoje Klasić, Tvrtko Jakovina and Dragan Markovina are its supporters. The terrorizing of the Croatian language continued until the unconstitutional Declaration of Common Language in 2017. The civil society is governed by proven Yugoslavs, funded externally and from the Croatian budget, and networking in the "Yugo-sphere." The most prominent are Zoran Pusić, Rada Borić, Vesna Teršelić, Dragan Zelić...

In such circumstances, the Serb national minority politicians do not accept minority status. The newsletter *Srbobran* [Serbo-fender] from the beginning of the last century was renamed as *Novosti* [News], and is edited as though the Serbs were owners of Croatia. That anti-Croatian newsletter is published in the middle of Zagreb. Although it is heavily financed by the Croatian budget, it continuously offends the Croats and Croatian state, depreciates Croatian institutions and attacks Croatian identity. The publisher is the privileged Serbian National Council led by the obligatory presence of Milorad Pupovac. Through multiple mandates already, he continues the job started by Nikola Stojanović, Svetozar Pribićević, continued by Aleksandar Ranković, Dušan Dragosavac, and Jovan Rašković. He has become the most powerful arbitrator in the country, even if he gains a minor number of votes in the elections. Croatian leading party politicians increasingly resemble those of the Yugoslav Committee and the National Council of a hundred years ago, who took the Croatian people and territories into a community with Serbia from which the Croatian people came out decimated, plundered and with half of their territory.

The Croatian people must ask themselves where the politicians have led them: Ivo Sanader, Stjepan Mesić, Ivo Josipović, Jadranka Kosor, Zoran Milanović, Andrej Plenković, Zlatko Tomčić, Vladimir Šeks, Luka Bebić, Boris Šprem, Josip Leko, Željko Reiner .... How was Croatia presented by Ministers of Foreign Affairs such as Vesna Pusić - who accuses Croatia of an imaginary aggression, or ambassadors like Ivo Goldstein, who represented Croatia in Paris with the photo of communist criminal Josip Broz Tito?

The last Yugoslav Republic Day was celebrated in The Hague on 29 November 2017, with the convicting verdict against a group of Croats from Bosnia and Herzegovina, whereby Croatia was declared the aggressor on Bosnia and Herzegovina. General Slobodan Praljak took his life in the courtroom with the cry "I reject your verdict with contempt."

As if it was not enough that the Greater Serbia and Yugoslav ideology were rehabilitated, Plenković's government also imposed gender ideology by ratifying the Istanbul Convention in 2018. Moreover, on 4 August 2018 in Bačka Palanka, Serbia and the Serbian Othodox Church, in the presence of Milorad Pupovac, compared Croatia to Hitler's Germany, creating a new myth about Operation Storm as a pogrom of Serbs.

Despite the systematic action of the Croatian fifth column embedded into the deep state - Croatia won second place in the 2018 World Football Cup and it showed to the denationalized political elites that it was a global subject, and not a Balkan object. The success was not hindered by the many years of anti-Croatian hysteria produced by the professional football informant from Rijeka, Zoran Stevanović. Alongside him is his fellow townsman Željko Jovanović. As Minister of the Croatian Government, he silently watched the burning of the Croatian flag at the Belgrade stadium. From his ministerial position, he carried out a number of diversions in the field of science, education and sports. The judicial institutions rejected all his "reforms". During the time of Minister Ranko Ostojić, a swastika dawned on the stadium in Split. To add to the humiliation, civil servants had to walk Minister Milanka Opačić's dog.

At the same time, the exiled government of the Republic of Serbian Krajina operates legally in Serbia, streets carry the names of prominent killers of Croats, Chetniks, aggressors and servants of the Greater Serbian politics. Chetniks become Presidents. Serbia and the Serb Orthodox Church are the only ones in the world who oppose the canonization of blessed Alojzije Stepinac. Even in the twenty-first century, Serbian state politics, as well as the Serbian Orthodox Church consider Croatia to be a temporarily lost Serbian country, which has to be "liberated" and "annexed" at a convenient moment. They are greatly assisted in their task by the Croatian fifth column of Yugoslav geese and Greater Serbian and communist snakes.

The Croatian people must defeat the Yugoslav, Greater Serbian and communist ideology in their country. Whether Croatia will reach the end of the twenty-first century as a free and sovereign political nation, or it will disappear from history, depends on that victory or defeat. Serbia holds the same political views toward Croatia in 2018 as those it held in 1918.

Belgrade's soul and brain new production

Croatia missed the opportunity to enter the essence of democratic society due to, among other things, failing to pass two lustration laws, and due to passing a large number of laws and loopholes in the law, which are harmful for the state and the nation. Today it is obvious even to incorrigible sceptics that it was necessary to pass a law on the lustration of communist remnants. And it was also necessary to pass a law on the lustration of Greater Serbian remnants.

Successful confrontation with the past of a myth

In a recent edition of the journal *Glas Koncila*, Tomislav Vuković published a new article titled *How the myth was created* (regarding 20,101 children killed in the Jasenovac camp). Vuković constantly erodes the system of myths built in the Yugo-communist regime that was strongly exploited during the preparation of the Greater Serbian aggression and is subversively maintained to the present day.

His previous book, *Different history* (Zagreb, 2012) released by the same publisher, did not go unnoticed even though the leading media remained silent. It contains a collection of leaflets that were published in *Glas Koncila* on topics which the non-lustrated remnants of the totalitarian regime, disguised as "anti-fascism", consider to be binding publication. *How the myth was created* is the continuation of Vuković's journalistic research work through which he became recognized among the Catholic and general public.

The topics that Vuković puts into focus are the myths on which Yugoslavia was built and under which Croatia groaned. The myths used to feed the Greater Serbian aggression on Croatia convincing everyone around and within of their truthfulness through agitprop. Contemporary Croatian politics, both party and media, did not carry out a systematic and argumented deconstruction of the myths inherited from totalitarianism. On the contrary, it allowed the creation of new myths that directly erode the foundations of the modern Croatian state. That is why this journalistic publication, strengthened by appendices and critical apparatus, is an important contribution to the elucidation of the truth and the deconstruction of ideologically motivated forgeries. Let us not be fooled by the fact that the leading media will give this book a wide berth. In our circumstances that is indeed a trustworthy sign that the book is worth the attention because it reveals the system of forgeries in the service of communist anti-fascism and Greater Serbian hatred.

The structure of the book consists of four chapters: Manipulations with the number of victims; How is it possible to falsify the lists of victims and to multiply their number several times; Manipulation of data about children in the camps; The unsuccessful search for mass graves. Each chapter has several interesting subtitles. Dr Vladimir Geiger reviewed the manuscript. From the critical review we learn how the number of "killed children" varies from one author to another and it reaches 29,000. However, "Vuković has made an effort in articulating and clearly making available all the most important information and explanations indispensable to understanding the intentions of the cataloguers and name lists, as well as the ways of manipulating the lists of Jasenovac victims... through text and attachments he complements the important unknowns in understanding the unavoidable questions of contemporary history, namely, the number of Jasenovac victims…".

In the Introduction, Ivan Miklenić points out that the book "enters only one segment of the incredibly vast and systematically extended and re-expanded myth about the Jasenovac camp" and adds that the book is also "an important contribution for the average reader, especially an intellectual or a historian, to confront the fact that the suffering in Jasenovac camp also served as basis for the creation of the myth, which no longer has almost anything left in common with the historical truth".

In the preface, the author emphasizes that the book could have been complemented with the chapter "How does a myth persist" because in the appendix "three additional texts have been published that show the shocking and quite incredibly extreme unscientific and manipulative effort of the JUSP Jasenovac[24] employees to frantically defend the indefensible – the above mentioned number of killed children".

The supplement to the book publicizes the text by Dr Stjepan Razum "I inform the Croatian public that I have discovered great fraud in Jasenovac", (one of the capital journalistic texts of recent times on busting and understanding the Jasenovac myth), previously published in the *Croatian Weekly* [*Hrvatski Tjednik*] of 11 June 2015, followed by the answer to that text by the person responsible in the Public Institution Memorial Area Jasenovac (interview with Zdenko Ćorić; The database contains the same victims as before 1 June, published in the *Croatian Weekly* of 2 July 2015), and by Dr Razum's reaction to the claims presented in the interview (The company Utilis attempts to cover-up Jasenovac fraud with tricks, *Croatian Weekly*, 2 July 2015).

---

24 *JUSP Jasenovac (Javna ustanova Spomen područje Jasenovac)* - Public
   Institution Memorial Area Jasenovac, established   1968.

One of the most impressive parts of the book, and I apologize for the subjectivity, refers to the sub-title "Chetniks and the 'popular homemade culture'". The text captured me with its freshness even when I read it probably for the second time. The freshness refers to the fact that at least once a year, official Croatian representatives bow to the Chetniks in Jasenovac. That is, the following. Vuković came up with information on how in the battle with the Ustasha "in the great battle in Lijevče Polje near Banja Luka, between 30 March and 8 April 1945" the Chetniks got a good and proper smack in the gob. And because it was just as it was, respected readers, you were not taught about this battle in school, nor do the media remind you about it every year on 8 April, as they do when it comes to the so-called "Uprising" in Srb[25].

"The General" Draža, however, was honest: "Lijevče Polje became the most tragic Serbian place of execution…". In short, the boys defeated the Chetniks in battle (the partisans were probably in the woods waiting for the Chetniks to turn into partisans and for the arrival of the "Red Army"). They captured "about 1,500 Chetniks with the commander "duke" Pavle Đurišić and his officer group, who were most likely taken and killed partly in the Stara Gradiška camp, and the rest in the Jasenovac camp".

Commander Đurišić was found on the "list of individual names of victims of the Jasenovac concentration camp" (page 444) with the following data: "Đurišić Pavle, 1907 - 1945, Titograd, Montenegrin, killed by the Ustasha in 1945 in the Jasenovac camp in an unconfirmed location". Not only him! There were also other butchers, "commanders": Major Petar Baćović, Major Luka Baletić, Colonel Zaharija Ostojić, and Major Dragiša Vasić. Meticulous Vuković wrote on the internet list that there were also the Chetnik Airforce Department Commander Miloš Dujović, the Gendarmerie Captain Petar Drašković, Commander of the Chetnik Attack Unit Andrija Drašković, Captain Gajo Radović. There

____

25 A rebellion led by Chetniks and Yugoslav Partisans against the Independent State of Croatia that started on 27 July 1941 in Srb, a village in the region of Lika, due to alleged persecutions of Serbs by the Ustasha. It soon spread across Lika and Bosanska Krajina and resulted in numerous war crimes committed against local Croat and Muslim population, especially in the area of Kulen Vakuf.

A century of Serbian terror 1918 - 2018

was no mention of how many "ordinary" attack, air force and gendarmerie Chetniks ended up in Jasenovac, out of the 1,500 captured fighters after the defeat in Lijevče Polje. And what is the point being made here?

It is the fact that official Croatia commemorates to this day even the Chetniks in Jasenovac! That is also the best illustration of the modern, non-lustrated, and partially "Chetnicised" Croatia. History repeats itself. There is, in fact, no register of Chetniks imprisoned in Jasenovac in 1945, or a register of Chetniks who participated in the Greater Serbian aggression on Croatia 1991-1998. Therefore, because the non-lustrated Party is still today in silent coalition with the non-lustrated Chetnik Movement, there will be occasional persistence of the myth of the "killed children", which Vuković dismantled in 160 pages into its component pieces. His book is, among other things, an excellent teaching aid for history teachers in elementary and middle schools, which unfortunately means also for the majority of the political elite in Croatia. Although its arguments "confronted us with the history" of the myth about the "killed children", I do not believe that it will enter the literature recommended by the "curricular reform".

(hkv.hr, 1 March 2016)

Draft for the legal action against the editors of the publication *Speech of Hatred and Violence Against Serbs in 2015*

In the editions of the Serbian National Council (SNV) and the Council of the Serbian National Minority of the City of Zagreb (VSNMGZ), the bilingual publication entitled SPEECH OF HATRED AND VIOLENCE AGAINST SERBS IN 2015 was produced and made public in March 2016. The publication was printed in 600 copies. It is also available on the internet. The author of the publication is not mentioned. The publication was edited by Saša Milošević, journalist and diplomat, assistant to Milorad Pupovac, President of SNV Association, and member of the Presidency of the SNV.

The publication, as the publishers point out, "brings a review of the cases of ethnically-motivated violence, threats and speech of hatred directed against Serbs in Croatia during the previous year". There are 189 cases "which were collected by the SNV and the Club of the SDSS Party[26] representatives from reports of individuals and information published in the media".

The publishers classified the cases collected by the SNV and the Club of the SDSS Party representatives into five thematic units. The first unit is entitled: "Elements of speech of hatred or the spread of ethnic intolerance in public." The first unit of the publication is divided into several sub-titles (smaller units). One of them is entitled "1.3. The Media", which on page 14 of the pdf internet edition begins with the subtitle "1.3.1. Electronic Media."

In that part of the publication which "brings a review of the cases of ethnically-motivated violence, threats and speech of hatred directed against Serbs in Croatia during the previous year", the following quotation was published on page 16 as an element of the speech of hatred or the spread of ethnic intolerance in public:

The events organized on the occasion of the anniversary of Operation Storm inspired the authors whose texts are published on the portal of the Croatian Cultural Council, hkv.hr. "This year's anti-Storm incidents directed by Pupovac, Teršelić, Džakula and Frljić are not only attacks on Operation Storm and what it symbolizes, but also on international criminal law. For this reason, the sabotage actions of the alternative and self-proclaimed 'celebration', marked by 'interactive presentation', gathered in Pješćanica (author's comment – the village in Vrginmost Municipality, where a commemorative gathering took place on 2 August in memory of civilians who were killed or disappeared in the Operation Storm) and on Ban Jelačić Square [Zagreb], as well as the abuse of the Croatian National Theatre in Rijeka, organized on the occasion of Belgrade's Remembrance Day of Storm Victims, can be considered as a subversion against the state, its constitutional system and the obstruction of public order and peace. These are the illegal acts that fall within the same class as the appearance of the swastika on the Poljud stadium and the attack on the *Croatian Weekly* newspaper in Zadar. Even in Bosnia and Herzegovina they belong

---

26 *SDSS (Samostalna demokratska srpska stranka)* – Independent Democratic Serb Party, founded 1997.

A century of Serbian terror 1918 - 2018

to the area from the other side of the law, which in every normal country falls within the jurisdiction of the repressive, judicial and prison systems" as stated in the text by Nenad Piskač published on that portal on 4 August (end of quote).

It is sheer imputation that the above quotation represents hatred, threat, violence or the spreading of ethnic intolerance.

The above is a small part of my text published on 4 August 2015 under the heading THE WAR AGAINST OPERATION STORM DESERVES LEGAL ACTION BY THE REPRESSIVE MECHANISM and under the title UNDERMINING THE FOUNDATIONS OF THE CROATIAN STATE IS UNPUNISHABLE AND PROFITABLE and the sub-title THE SCOPE OF THE REPRESSIVE AND JUDICIAL MECHANISM. The entire text is available on the hkv.hr portal.

It is visible from the above that my text, published on the portal of the Croatian Cultural Council:

1. Is the subject of denunciation by anonymous individuals

2. That the denunciation by anonymous individuals was forwarded to the Serbian National Council and to the Club of SDSS Party representatives, instead of relevant institutions of the Republic of Croatia

3. That my text was subjected to group "analysis" by the SNV and the Club of SDSS Party representatives, that is, an association of citizens and the three-member section of the Croatian Assembly

4. That without my knowledge, part of the text was taken out of context and printed with a translation into English for the purpose of international denunciation of the author and of the electronic medium

5. That the text was labeled both as a "threat" and as "spread of ethnic intolerance" and classified among the 189 alleged cases of speech of hatred and violence against Serbs in 2015

6. That the detached piece was undoubtedly published in the controversial publication and on the internet.

In short, my text appeared on a wanted person warrant. Since the author of the warrant is not mentioned in the imprint, I consider the publishers of the publication responsible for the consequences.

On the basis of my complete text and the printed fragment, and the context in which the text, the fragment, the author and the electronic medium were placed, it undoubtedly follows:

1. That the publishers of the publication consider that the war against Operation Storm does not deserve the action of the repressive mechanism, and that the undermining of the foundations of the Croatian state must remain unpunishable and profitable. Whoever within the public domain thinks the opposite automatically deserves the label - ethnically motivated speech of hatred, coercion and violence against the Serbs in Croatia, that is – the public spread of ethnic intolerance.

2. That the publishers believe last year's anti-Storm incidents directed by Pupovac, Teršelić, Džakula and Frljić, inspired by the "Remembrance Day of Storm Victims" (officially proclaimed in the neighbouring state), not to have been attacks on the military and police Operation Storm and the International Criminal Law, which cleared Operation Storm of any kind of stigma and the unfounded charges of a joint criminal venture of expelling Serbs from Croatia, but that whoever writes differently in public is automatically subject on behalf of the SNV and VSNMGZ to international condemnation for the speech of hatred, coercion and violence against the Serbs in Croatia, that is – the spread of ethnic intolerance in public.

3. The publishers consider that the repressive, judicial and prison systems of the Republic of Croatia should not deal with the perpetrators of crimes of subversive activities against the state, its constitutional system and the disturbance of public order and peace in the way that all other democratic and ordered states do, and those who think and act contrary to that are automatically and without a valid verdict guilty of the speech of hatred, coercion and violence against the Serbs in Croatia, that is - the spread of ethnic intolerance in public.

The views of the publishers are in fact, not those of a sane mind, but that does not free them of their responsibilities. The publishers have, therefore, rigged the detached fragment of my text in single-party, single-ethnic, single-minded manner, labeled it in totalitarian fashion, translated it without permission, published it malevolently, placed and interpreted it internationally as:

a) speech of hatred towards Serbs in Croatia

b) threats and violence towards Serbs in Croatia

c) spread of ethnic intolerance

The truth is, however, that in the text I advocate the rule of law, and I do not mention in that fragment "Serbs in Croatia", nor anything that could be considered as speech of hatred, threats, violence or the spread of ethnic intolerance. On the contrary, I point at the speech of hatred, threats, violence and the spread of ethnic intolerance in the public domain of the Republic of Croatia and in wider neighbouring areas.

The publishers, SNV and VSNMGZ, have mislead the domestic and world public through the released publication. They calumniated and inflicted incalculable damage to the author of the text and to the medium which published it. It is uncontestable, in fact, that neither the author N. Piskač nor the electronic medium hkv.hr were charged for transgression or penalty regarding the mentioned text, nor was there any dispute against them due to that text or any part of the text. During the past eight months, nobody has issued an official denial of the text as a whole or any part of the text.

The author rightly considers that in his case it is a matter of ethnical, single-party, single-ethnical and a totalitarian style attack by SNV and VSNMGZ on his personal integrity, his Croatian nationality, his human, professional and war veteran's dignity, the honour and reputation that he enjoys as a Croat, Croatian citizen, columnist, writer and Croatian veteran, as well as an attack on the reputation and credibility of the electronic medium in which he has been publishing for years. Moreover, it is a question of a perfidious speech of hatred, a subtle threat, and indisputable violation, which ultimately represents the attack by the mentioned publishers, and partly by the SDSS Party, on the freedom of speech and thought warranted by the Constitution of the Republic of Croatia, with the intention to create, with a controversial publication, a false impression in the local and foreign communities of how Serbs are endangered in Croatia and thus cause damage to the international reputation of the Republic of Croatia which, in my opinion, is the ultimate aim of the publication. Croatian historiography has scientifically dealt with the myth of endangered Serbs in Croatia, therefore, there is no need to additionally explain it here, however, the work of Croatian historians on that topic will be welcome in legal witness proceedings.

The calumniated author expresses solidarity with other people, beginning with the President of the Republic of Croatia, Mrs. Kolinda Grabar-Kitarović, who also appeared, as he did, through malicious and special warfare methods, in the controversial publication of SNV and VSNMGZ. I invite my slandered journalist colleagues to come together in a joint lawsuit and I suggest a parallel private law suit. Without a court verdict this practice will continue.

Therefore, I inform the public that this text is a draft for a private suit against the publisher. Single-ethnical, single-party, politically and ethno-commercially motivated violence was committed against me. My text was used for anti-Croatian activity. Since the calumniated author does not have the knowledge and skills necessary to institute legal proceedings, he invites lawyers, local and those abroad, regardless of their nationality, to contact him if they should wish to file a *pro bono* trial process. *Pro bono* because the author (like the medium in which he publishes), unlike the SNV, VSNMGZ and the SDSS is not on an abundant state provided budget.

Regardless of the announced private and potential joint lawsuit, the author, calumniated locally and abroad, invites the relevant state services to get out of their snail shell and in their official duty, without fear of anyone, get to work in discovering and processing anti-Croatian activities, especially those financed with Croatian funds. THE SPEECH OF HATRED AND VIOLENCE AGAINST SERBS IN 2015 is a radical example of the spreading of ethnic intolerance. I am surprised that this escaped the eye of the editor Saša Milošević.

(hkv.hr, 10 March 2016)

A century of Serbian terror 1918 - 2018

Pupovac's report to Belgrade is riddled with inaccuracies

While the anti-Croatian campaign in Serbia has not stopped since the eighties of the last century, the best-known ethno-businessman "in these regions" is perturbing the Serb public on Serbian media with the fabrication that Croatia has returned to the nineties. It would be excellent if this were true! Croatia is now, unlike in the nineties, a member of NATO and the EU. Compared to the nineties, Croatia has become a state heavily in debt, from which the Croats emigrate and to which the EU imposes a so-called migrant quota. Croatia was a regional power in the nineties. Today it is mentally "part of the territory of former Yugoslavia" in which Pupovac has become a privileged arbiter. Since 3 January 2000, the politics of a rebounding communist wave and the betrayal of national politics have transformed Croatia from being a subject to being an object. Anguish and despair have been installed in place of the pride of the nineties.

Croatia did not return to the nineties but to the eighties. Had Croatia returned to the nineties, it would be a stable state, it would have a stable government with a semi-presidential system in which it is clear who is responsible for what. Had Croatia returned to the nineties, Milorad Pupovac would be an ordinary citizen and not a political factor with the task to act as a prosthetic extension of Belgrade politics. Had Croatia returned to the splendid nineties, Pupovac could not publish once a year the Greater Serbian arrest warrant against persons of different views. Croatia has, firstly through betrayal, and then with his own unselfish help, returned to the eighties.

The second part of his argument that Croatia has returned to the nineties and renewed the anti-Serbian campaign is also incorrect. It is the Greater Serbian anti-Croatian campaign that has been renewed in Croatia, which always begins with reviving the thesis on a "century of threats". The political leaders of Serbs in Croatia actually insist on that thesis. While the main threat lies in the fact that Greater Serbia was not extended up to Virovitica, Karlovac and Karlobag, but only up to Banja Luka.

It is incorrect that "the new Government has completely excluded Serbs and other minorities from its program, and included only the extreme right and the extremely conservative groups". The new government did not include or exclude anyone. It did not even take over the power of the past government, which had completely excluded the Croats from its Program 21, and which included the extreme left and extremely liberal groups, and established them as professional parasites on the Croatian budget so long as they work in its interests.

The argument that "the situation has deteriorated with Croatia's joining the European Union" is incorrect. The situation in Croatia dramatically deteriorated on 3 January 2000. It deteriorated not only for the Serbian national minorities, but for all citizens of the Republic of Croatia. The situation further deteriorated when Pupovac became a factor of authority in the Croatian-Serbian government of Ivo Sanader. Pupovac is an unavoidable part of the general worsening of the situation in Croatia.

It is incorrect that "civil resistance" weakens the "wave of the extreme Right and of historical revisionism". The resistance mentioned in Pupovac's Belgrade interview is not civil, but neo-communist. It undermines the stability of the Croatian Government and it calls for the return to the past, to the sixth worst government in the world, or at least one like that led by Sanader.

Pupovac's mention of the HDZ and the Catholic Church in the context of the need for their contribution to weaken the wave of right extremism and historical revisionism represents political extortion. According to all objective indicators, there is no extremism of the right in Croatia. The increasingly loud attempts for the historical truth to be determined outside of the ideological, communist Greater Serbia, represents historical revisionism only for the communists and Greater Serbs. It would be good that Pupovac explains the role of the Serbian Orthodox Church in strengthening the wave of Greater Serbian extremism and historical revisionism.

Only the rotten remnants of the failed Yugo-communist regime can see an open clerical and national totalitarianism in Croatia today. This did not exist even in the nineties. However, it did exist on the Serbian side in the eighties and the nineties. The statements of top officials in the Serbian Orthodox Church, Serbian political leadership and the rebel wing of Serbs in Croatia are the best witnesses to that. Pupovac forgot them, just as he forgot the fate of Dr. Ivan Šreter[27].

The undisturbed protests against Minister Hasanbegović and the absurd protest against everything and in favor of nothing in the Square [of Ban Jelačić in Zagreb], are the best proof regarding the alleged return of Croatia to the nineties, and the alleged clerical and national totalitarianism in Croatia. Nevertheless, Pupovac uses them in his media offerings as an argument to prove "right-wing primitivism". Oh, how primitive!

The Greater Serbian primitivism is, in this case, a repetition of the same anti-Croatian tactics about the "centuries of endangering Serbian children", which is present in the foundation of the Greater Serbian aggression. However, the great Croatian primitivism is that Croatia does not react to the Greater Serbian tactics in principle and in accordance with the historical truth on the political, legislative and judicial level. This is the clearest indication that Croatia was pushed into the mental state of the eighties. For this reason, the statement that "Croatia has a tendency towards rehabilitating also the forties of the twentieth century" deserves a proceeding by the State Prosecutor's Office, but also the condemnation by the political parties, the President of the Croatian Parliament, the President of the Croatian Government and President of the Republic of Croatia.

Pupovac proved with his interview that he is ready for the theses on Greater Serbia. The theories of Greater Serbia are the basis for all his accusations of Croatia. All of them! They take us back to the years of Yugo-communism, which are considered in Serbia as the years of Greater Serbia, only under another name. Their repetition represents the renewal of the anti-Croatian campaign, and they are the pledge of a future attack. They are the expression and reflection of the clericalism of Greater Serbia and Saint Sava. They are the Greater Serbian left and right primitivism, both here and in Serbia. Their disclosure and representation constituted the tendency of rehabilitation and permanent establishment of the Chetnik Movement, of national totalitarianism, and of the Belgrade forties all the way to the

---

27 Dr. Ivan Šreter (1951-1991) was a Croatian physician who was persecuted by Yugoslav authorities for using the Croatian language and killed by Serbs in 1991 in the Croatian Homeland War for independence.

nineties of the twentieth century. Finally, they are a justification for the aggression committed and an introduction to the non-existent "civil war".

The rehabilitation of the non-existent threats to Serbs is the return to the initial position of the Greater Serbian aggression on Croatia. However, in just one aspect, Pupovac is right in his claims that Croatia has returned to the nineties. Croatia returned and surpassed the nineties in terms of the deaths of Croatian war veterans. The longer Pupovac (and not only him) is a political tutor and arbiter of the Croatian society, the more they die.

According to the data of the Coordination of War Veterans Associations of the Croatian royal town of Knin, the situation is worse than in wartime. In 2009, an average of five Croatian veterans died daily, a total of 1,890. In 2012, an average of six Croatian veterans died daily, a total of 2,354. In 2015, eight Croatian veterans died daily, a total of 2.955. The average life span of Croatian veterans is 50.9 years. The average lifespan in Croatia is 76 years of age.

Who, then, is actually threatened in Croatia?! During the first four months of 2016, ten Croatian veterans died each day, a total of 1,085. The mortality of Croatian veterans today is almost ten times greater than in wartime. During the eight years of the Greater Serbian aggression, 6,891 Croatian defenders were killed at an average of 0.4 per day. Today the number is ten! We have surpassed the nineties by more than 9.5 deceased veterans per day, but we have not yet exceeded the May 1945 - March 1951 period. Pupovac did not report on this to Belgrade.

(hkv.hr, 7 June 2016)

British deceit: Vučić is the anchor of stability in the region

Thirty years have passed since the public release of the strategic imperial Serbian document of the Serbian Academy of Sciences and Arts, entitled Memorandum (*Evening News*, 24-25 September 1986). Twenty-five years have also passed since the glorious send-off of the JNA First Guard Armoured Division from Belgrade in the direction of Vukovar (19 September 1991), the city where its teeth were broken, and in Operation Storm its backbone too.

And while these days we remember the two anniversaries, the London *Economist* wrote (on 17 September, the day after the 25th anniversary of the flower strewn send-off of "Tito's elite Division"), carefully appraised and chosen panegyrics to Aleksandar Vučić, head of the Serbian Government, the person who participated, on the basis of the Memorandum and the Belgrade flower-decked caterpillar vehicles of Tito's Division, in the Greater Serbian aggression on Croatia (and later that on Bosnia and Herzegovina and on Kosovo). The London newspaper wrote "as a Europhile, the former ultranationalist Aleksandar Vučić is the biggest surprise to Europe." Did the Vučić – Blair axis begin to work?

Vučić engaged Tony Blair (in 2015) as an advisor with the aim to lobby for Serbian interests and to bring the unpunished Serbia closer to the European Union. This cooperation was established despite the fact that Vučić was the editor (allegedly also reviewer) of the book *English Gay Fart Tony Blair* (2005), written by Vojislav Šešelj. With this book, Greater Serbian Belgrade got even with Blair for the fact that under his leadership Great Britain participated in the NATO attack on Serbia when Vučić was Milošević's Minister of Information and Serbia lost the position of being the Yugoslav "educative baton".[28]

Today, however, despite the circumstances of the British referendum regarding the exit from the EU, and those in which the EU is not keen on further expansion, it is apparent from the context of the article that Great Britain and (Greater) Serbia are not renouncing on the century-old British foreign policy "in this area", that is, in the "region", or "on these territories", more precisely in the "Yugo-sphere" laboratory located on the geographically non-existent "Western Balkans". That is, the territory on which Serbia is continually losing expansionist wars, but does not give up on its imperial politics and the role of first "baton" to the south and east of the Virovitica-Karlovac-Karlobag line.

The *Economist* praises Vučić, it builds him up to European stature and states that his main strategic goal is to secure Serbia's entry into the European Union. No, his main goal is to free Serbia of the responsibility for imperialist wars and the great crimes committed in them. Of those who remind him of "his days when he was a bitter ultranationalist",

---

28 *Vaspitna palica* – school cane; in Serb jargon a police truncheon

Vučić says: "They live in the 1990's" - writes the London newspaper, without noticing how, thanks to Vučić, Serbia is also lagging behind in the 1990's. However, the newspaper continues, "Vučić is basking in the sun". Why wouldn't he, when the "Western leaders" consider Mr Vučić to be, according to the words of the Austrian Minister of Foreign Affairs Sebastian Kurz, "an anchor of stability in that region."

In addition to Great Britain and the little Greater Serbia, it seems that also the short-sighted "Western leaders" are installing the new Milošević in Serbia, and indirectly also the new Karadžić in Bosnia and Herzegovina, while the new Jovan Rašković was installed in Croatia with their help already in 2004. Pupovac has been playing the role of the bearded psychiatrist in Croatia for a long time. Still, there are differences. Tuđman fired Rašković, but Tuđman's successors are paying Pupovac. We could illustrate this situation jokingly like this - Milorad Rašković was in charge of implementing the goals of Memorandum 1 in Croatia. Jovan Pupovac is in charge of the goals of Memorandum 2, and the "Western leaders" are in charge of both.

At the beginning of the nineties, Slobodan Milošević was the anchor of stability and preservation of Yugoslavia in the eyes of Western leaders. He did not succeed, even with the help of Tito's devilish Divisions. Therefore, the current process of installing a new Serbian leader is no surprise from Europe. True, this time the current process of installing substitute leaders began from the periphery (Zagreb, Banja Luka) towards the centre (Belgrade). But their purpose is the same. In the moment the new formation of Serb leaders gets a public blessing from the Serbian Orthodox Church, the cohesive "spiritual" force of the Greater Serbian politics, a new aggression will be ready on the political level at the nod of the "Western leaders" for classic or "asymmetrical" (D.D. Lošo[29] "action". Just as it was in 1990-1991.

---

29 Croatian Admiral Davor Domazet Lošo describes an 'asymmetric' war as one without soldiers, a start date, a battleground or a battle, but nevertheless a war intended to endanger or conquer a territory, in this case that between Boka Kotorska, Herzegovina and Dalmatia, which is populated by Croats because without Herzegovina and Dalmatia there will be no Croatia.

A century of Serbian terror 1918 - 2018

The extreme Serbian politics is helped by the uninterested, short-sighted and impotent politics of the majority of European Union countries, but especially by the post-Tuđman anti-politics of the Croatian state, which has been carried out by trained or bought *chargé d'affaires* ever since Račan. Because of that, the developments in Serbia are of paramount importance to Croatian foreign and internal politics, but also because Pupovac, as leader of Serbs in Croatia who are not rebelled at the moment, is very frequently meeting and aligning with the Chetniks Vučić and Nikolić, while at the same time and without any resistance significantly arbitrating in Croatia.

What is the main current in Serbia in relation to the Memorandum? The *Economist* rushed to praise Vučić at the time when Serbia put into high gear the policy of justifying, exalting, evoking and fully rehabilitating both the Memorandum and the Greater Serbian aggression. Also, at the time when in occupied Banja Luka the "referendum with 99.8 percent" confirmed 9 January (1992) as the "Day of the Serbian Republic", giving the genocide in the name of Greater Serbia the right to sovereignty (alongside the "annexing" to Belgrade). With the help of the "referendum" (carried out partially according to the principles of the "yogurt revolution"[30], partially according to Milošević's instructions – "institutionally and non-institutionally"), the Greater Serbianism is, among other, trying to create in Dodik a new and reliable Radovan Karadžić.

Was the solitary voice of Belgrade historian Latinka Perović right when she recently said that Serbia is not returning to the nineties since it mentally never even stepped out of the imperialist wars of those times? If we are to believe politicians, academicians, and the media - the spirit of the times in Serbia is spinning in a circle. Thus, the *Nedjeljnik* newspaper, when writing extensively about the anniversary of the first Memorandum,

---

30 *"Jogurt revolucija"* – ' the yoghurt revolution', or the 1988-1989 Anti-Bureaucratic Revolution of street protests in Vojvodina, when protesters hurled yogurt cartons onto Party officials who tried to calm the situation. It marked the centralisation of Milošević' Serbia and constitutional amendments that cut off Vojvodina and Kosovo's autonomy within the former Yugoslavia, and eventually resulted in the dissolution of the League of Communists of Yugoslavia in 1990, and subsequently in the break up of SFR Yugoslavia.

transmitted the message of Vladimir Kostić, president of SANU, who claims that the Memorandum was not accepted, stating that it was a matter of a dangerous construction and a heavy mortgage imposed on SANU. Vasilije Krestić, a well-known Greater Serbia academician, claims that the attacks on the Memorandum are unfounded creations of those who are tearing Yugoslavia apart.

The *Informer*, the most widely read newspaper in Serbia and the yellow press that generally transmits what the Serbian political top and the local informer community think, sends very positive messages about the Memorandum. The newspaper *Večernje novosti* transmits similar messages. When speaking about the Memorandum, Editor-in-Chief Ratko Dmitrović, a former well-known Greater Serbia media agitator, states that SANU has to get rid of the great lie that it was the laboratory of evil.

The Helsinki Committee for Human Rights in Serbia also spoke about the role of SANU. The Committee condemned the rehabilitation of imperialist war politics of Serbia relating to the periods of preparation and execution of the Greater Serbian aggressions. It warns about the attempt to fully absolve Serbia of any responsibility for former creators of the Greater Serbian politics. The Committee also condemned the silence of the Serbian society. It concludes that Serbia had entered the conquest wars in the nineties by consensus, and that with a high degree of consent, it accepts those criminal politics as correct and justified today.

With reference to SANU, the Helsinki Committee argues that Serbia's role in preparing the war and war propaganda belongs to the category of historical facts, and not that of personal beliefs. It points out that in Serbia and abroad, many scientific papers, documents, testimonies and evidence have been published, which undoubtedly reveal the truth about the historical role of SANU and its responsibility for the wars. In Serbia, however, there is a constant reheating of myths and production of historical forgeries, instead of a break-off with the dark side of the Greater Serbian politics.

The current and former Serbian politicians and most of the media, do not allow Serbia to emerge from the dense opium fog of the Greater Serbian flowers of evil. Last summer, Ivica Dačić, the "little Slobo" and post-Milošević officer of the Serbian Socialist Party and current Foreign

Affairs Minister, presented the Ministry's official view, hence that of the Serbian Government, that The Hague verdict against Karadžič acquitted Milošević of the war crimes allegations, of ethnic cleansing and genocide. That the charges against Milošević, Serbia and SR Yugoslavia were false. Despite all known and unknown evidence.

Minister Aleksandar Vulin (entrusted with raising tensions towards Croatia), who collaborated with Mira Marković and her "Yugoslav Left" during the nineties, considers that The Hague Tribunal has attested that the Serbian nation was just, that the politics of that time was correct, that Serbia did not lead or cause any wars, but rather that the wars were imposed upon Serbia. Meaning, for example, that Croatia was responsible for the Greater Serbian aggression in Croatia.

The Greater Serbian protagonist from the nineties, Borislav Jović published the book "How the Serbs Lost a Century." In that book he laments, like the SANU Memorandum thirty years earlier, the tragic fate of Serbs in Yugoslavia. In the "Kurir" interview Jović reports the known Greater Serbian claims: The war was imposed on Serbia, Serbs are not responsible for the wars, in the nineties Serbs were defending their land, Serbs were deceived, Serbs were victims and they were systematically deprived of their rights – and they believed in brotherhood and unity. He adds that Milošević had no choice, Serbia does not have to raise a monument to meritorious Milošević immediately, and that The Hague tribunal was given the task to punish Belgrade with the loss of the state....

Nikola Šainović, former President of the Serbian Government and Deputy Prime Minister of SR Yugoslavia, a Milošević admirer and charged suspect in The Hague Tribunal, a war criminal, spoke to the newspaper *Danas* with the proposal that Serbia must raise a monument to Milošević because of his contribution in the defense from aggression. Even the primitive Serbian-Australian terrorist Dragan Vasiljković shared the views of the Serbian intellectual elite. He was brought to the Court in Croatia on charges of practical implementation of the goals of the SANU Memorandum. At the trial he declared that he was not guilty, that he was only "defending Yugoslavia." Neither he, nor the rest of the Greater Serbia ventriloquists explained why he was "defending" Yugoslavia if the Serbs in Yugoslavia were "endangered" and had "lost a century" in it.

The Serbs are "endangered" again, though no longer in Yugoslavia, but in all Serbian "regions" scattered in the fogs of the British-Serbian "Yugosphere". During Yugoslavia the "regions" were "underdeveloped areas" for which solidarity funds were being set aside for decades. The more was invested in them the more underdeveloped they were. Pupovac's politics follow the communist politics for underdeveloped areas. He is asking for money even today, and if he does not get the amount he wants, then it's a case of "fascistisation of Croatia". However, not even an f of fascism exists in Croatia. But there is fascism in Serbia, where Pupovac marks 5 August as "Remembrance Day of Serbian Victims of Operation Storm", instead of marking it in Knin as Homeland Thanksgiving Day and the Day of Croatian War Veterans, while in return, during Orthodox Christmas for years now he successfully lines up the Croatian political-elite that are extremely submissive to him. He tells them: heel! They reply: Hristos [Christ in Serbian] is born!

Serbian President Tomislav Nikolić, former Šešelj's radical, participant in the Greater Serbian aggression on Croatia, who is legitimately suspected for taking part in crimes against civilians in the Croatian village of Antin, a Chetnik "duke", is an extremist of the Greater Serbian fascist thinking - all Serbs in one state. He openly admitted that the Greater Serbia is his unaccomplished dream, and that Kosovo vanished right before his eyes. He considers that Vukovar is a Serbian town, that Stepinac is a criminal and that the myth about Jasenovac is justification for imperialistic politics and mass crimes. He is the elected President of Serbia.

The *Economist's* "Europhile" and "Mister" Aleksandar Vučić, mastered the political lianas of the Greater Serbian politics in the nineties, by bringing crates of warm beer to Šešelj, Nikolić and other thirsty Chetniks. He participated in the Greater Serbian aggressions. He believes that Glina is Serbian territory, although it is a territory of the European Union ever since Croatia "returned home" (J. Kosor). He is a proven verbal and practical extremist. Even if he renounced Šešelj's and Milošević's fascism, he is a "former fascist". Milošević's agitprop (Minister of "Information"), he recently stated that Serbs would never accept Stepinac's canonization. He regularly wins in elections in Serbia.

Latinka Perović is right. Serbia did not step outside the Greater Serbian concept. Nothing else can be concluded after an insight into their local election results, where the most rigorous extremists and the most radical parties win, and after an insight into the character of its former and current government, into its poisoned media space, and into the rather stupid appearances of its "apprentices" and "artists". Serbia is ready for a new destabilization of the "territory of former Yugoslavia". Perhaps even an armed one. Its role in the "Yugosphere" laboratory is defined long-term as Greater Serbian. With regard to that, Serbia is now very well staffed in Belgrade, as well as in "Serbian regions" and "Serbian borders". A possible problem is only the historical memory, which the London *Economist* did not take into account when they promoted the proven follower of fascist politics to a Europhile.

Tuđman left Croatia poised as a regional power and a strong anchor of stability. Over the past sixteen years, the dismantlers of the Croatian state have done everything so that Croatia gives up on itself. By returning it to the eighties, they made it into an incompetent regional socialist republic that replaced brotherhood and unity with political correctness. Step by step, Croatia is renouncing not only sovereignty over the vital sectors of sustainable survival, but also the historical memory of the Greater Serbian aggression and its consequences. On anniversaries that cannot as yet be ignored, here and there a mention is made of the Homeland War being the foundation of the modern state of Croatia, but as a rule the Greater Serbian aggression and the name of the aggressors are avoided.

The Croatian political elites fool themselves in believing it is enough that Croatia is a member of the EU and NATO in order to parry with the Serbian "knife sharpening". Historical experience has taught us that key members of the EU and NATO have extradited Croatia into the jaws of the SANU Memorandum and pushed it under the caterpillar tracks of Greater Serbian fascism. Croatia defended itself from the intended expulsion from history only because Tuđman and the Croatian war veterans relied on "their own strength and on God's help." All subsequent politics have considerably contributed to the incursion of Greater Serbian politics by dulling resistance towards it. The Greater Serbian imperialist politics spanning from Milošević to Vučić are equally dangerous for national security as are the Croatian anti-politics with their head down, hands behind the back stance.

(hkv.hr, 27 September 2016)

The Synergy of Plenković's Committee and Pupovac's Bulletin

The Government's choice of officials forming the Committee on Confronting Consequences of Totalitarian Regimes and the false image of Croatia in the Serbian Bulletin perfectly complement each other. It is a matter of synergy between new Yugo-communism and the Greater Serbian Chetnik Movement. Yugo-communism and the Chetnik Movement share a common view – no independent state of Croatia. And should it be created, then it is to a certain degree fascist, and the entire Croatian nation has to permanently bear the consequences until it disappears from the historical scene. Fascism will disappear from Croatia when the state of Croatia and the Croats disappear. All principles of the internal blockade of sustainable development for Croatia have recently been sublimated with Plenković's staffing of the Committee and the announcement of Pupovac's indictment verdict. Not long ago the relevant services announced that there is an increase in left-wing extremism and in the Chetnik Movement in our country. However, the real extremists are creating an opposite image. As though there is an increase in right-wing extremism and Ustasha Movement, and they, poor dears – are innocent. And, of course, also endangered! Although the third generation now, by inheritance right, they suckle the state budget while working to our detriment.

Democratic Croatia should firstly face its current situation, and only then could it effectively face all the totalitarianisms that have drained it throughout the twentieth century: Greater Serbianism, fascism, Yugo-communism, then Greater Serbianism again, and finally the newest strange forms of insincere Europeanism with its Yugo-fingers crossed in its pocket. In view of the fact that we in Croatia can only make a significant step forward once we start calling things by their true names, as we did in the period between 1990 and 2000, when we broke the Croatian silence and we told a communist that he was a communist and we told a Chetnik that he was a Chetnik, it is logical and historically proven that we will not stop driving in neutral until we start calling things by their names again, as Dr. Ante Starčević wrote long ago. The impotent political correctness is of no use!

Instead of facing Dr Starčević the Croats are now facing Dr Pupovac. Instead of facing Dr Tuđman the Croats now face his poor surrogates, the

A century of Serbian terror 1918 - 2018

ones who carry out a reduced version of the SKH-SDP Party policies. Yes, until we begin to call things by their real names, we cannot face the present, not even the deformed electoral legislature, or the communist law on abortion, let alone the past.

Let us try to find the right name for Plenković's Committee panel and Pupovac's Bulletin. These are the two ends of the same pair of forceps used for the lobotomy of the Nation and the State. Both ends call for European values (inclusion and anti-fascism), but they actually carry out the old-Yugoslav and Yugo-communist violent imposition of the creative lie about which Dobrica Ćosić wrote anthological sentences in his book *Divisions*. Resistance to the policies of creative lies is now declared as populism and fascism.

The composition of the Committee panel has taken us back to the achievements of the Socialist Union of the Working People [SSRN] of Croatia. While the content and character of the Bulletin of a Single-nation Association of Citizens, SNV, which is a copy of the Yugoslav Self-management of Interest Communities, has already been seen and tested a hundred times during the last century as the base to stage processes against Croats and their State - institutionally and non-institutionally. All of that according to the recipe "until we or you are investigated" dated 1902, which is actualized in the poem *We will be chasing-up each other again* [*Ćeraćemo se još*] by SANU academician Matija Bećković, published, and not by chance, in 1996, after the Croatian Operation Storm.

Just as the SSRN has never resolved anything, but rather only served the Party to carry out its totalitarian politics more easily on the entire territory, so also Plenković's Committee, judging by its composition, will not solve anything except strengthen the ramparts of social divisions between the still privileged pro-Yugoslav communist elite (the "red bourgeoisie" and their descendants) and the Croatian majority. Pupovac's Bulletin does not resolve anything either, even if for ten consecutive years now he has been accusing the Croats and Croatia in the same manner as they were accused in the twentieth century by the Kingdom of Yugoslavia, Serbian Orthodox Church, SANU, KPH-SKJ all the way up to current Serbian Chetniks Nikolić, Vulin, Dačić, Vučić, Šešelj and their Croatian exponents.

The effects of the politics of establishing committees and agitprop bulletins nevertheless do exist. The politics of the SSRNH and the politics to stage processes following examples of Tito's and OZN[31] agitprop create a critical crowd of people for a new mass movement. Party members would call it a "massmov". It will be a reaction, like all national attempts until now, to break away from the biggest fallacy in Croatian national history. That is, that Croats can be converted into Serbs and that the spirit and brain of Belgrade can be forcibly imposed on Zagreb. The actions carried out in the spirit of SSRNH and actions carried out in the spirit of Greater Serbian politics cannot pass without a reaction. Especially if they are performed in synergy with the conspicuous execution of the politics of Croatian silence. True, as a rule the Croats are slow to react to anti-Croatian actions.

Let's not forget: even Pavelić was primarily a reaction to the terror of Greater Serbia politics of monarchist Yugoslavia. He reacted in 1929 to the continuation of Greater Serbia policies started in 1918 only when Croatian representatives were murdered by the Greater Serbs in 1928 in the Belgrade Parliament. Pavelić was the consequence, but the Greater Serbia politics was the cause. There was also a reaction to the Novi Sad agreement with the Declaration on the Name and Status of the Croatian Literary Language and Krleža was dismissed because of that....There was also a reaction in 1971....

There followed a felling of Croats and the installation of "the Croatian silence". The felling of Croats was all the greater the more violent and fruitful their reaction. That is the rule we carry forward from the experience in the Yugoslav community. However, the felling of Croats in 1972 is nothing compared to the scale of the felling of Croats that was carried out after 3 January 2000!

The only proper reaction to the Greater Serbian and Yugo-communist actions that resulted in permanent benefit happened in 1991, under the leadership of Dr Franjo Tuđman. That is why it also ended

---

31 OZNa *(Odjeljenje za zaštitu naroda)* - The Department for People's Protection, the security agency of Communist Yugoslavia that existed between 1944 and 1952.

A century of Serbian terror 1918 - 2018

in an overall de-Croatisation and de-Tuđmanisation. Not even one per cent of the lustrated, fired, trampled-down, harassed, processed and labeled Croats, who created the state but who were mowed down after 3 January 2000 in diplomacy, the military service, police, culture, media, state administration, state companies, local self-government, have been rehabilitated…. Among other indicators, the Croatian Army bore the brunt, as seen by the number of suicides among war veterans, which is more than frightening - it is difficult to win a defensive war, but it is even more difficult to lose in peace. The Croatian Army went through the worst also when we fell under the communist liberation of 1945.

I say there will be a reaction again because the state is being ridden by forces that have lost the imposed war on the Croats. It is impossible not to see that those very forces are the main brake for the State and the Nation. The reaction will happen when we start naming things, events, arbiters and phenomena by their real name and we put them into the verified historical context, and not into unleavened discussions of political committees and single-nation bulletins. In order to delay this process further into the future, Croats were deprived of their media, banks, political parties and existential security. In return they got debt slavery in their state and free emigration from it, but also the time-wasting committees in combination with the creative lies of Greater Serbian agitation and propaganda. Both are paid from the Croatian state budget. Clearly, this unsustainable situation cannot be maintained indefinitely without repression, violence and a combination of soft and hard forms and methods of totalitarianism.

Let us face the contemporary situation in order to be able to face the past. I did not check, but I am sure that when the Germans faced their past, they did not take any of Hitler's followers into their "committee". When in 1989 the Romanians faced their past, they did not appoint any fans of Ceausescu's image and deeds into their committees. Yet when Croats supposedly faced their past twenty-eight years after the Romanians, they appointed communist ideologists into the Committee, even oncologists, and persons who even today promote Tito whose army, with the five-pointed red star supported by the Chetnik cockade, committed the aggression on Croatia. They did it twice! The first time they literally decimated the whole nation.

Any confrontation is in total blockade - from the left, from the right and from the circles of Greater Serbia. What offers a glimmer of hope in all this relates to the law of physics - every action provokes a reaction, or as people colourfully described it long before Newton's Third Law of Motion – "Every arse gets to the privy". Hope is corroborated also by the unwritten law of Croatian national history as it was lived in the Yugoslav community – a Croat reacts only when his enemy literally crosses his threshold. This is why contemporary enemies, knowing the history of Croatian reactions to enemy actions, dose their operations so as to create a continuous atmosphere of low anti-Croatian intensity, in order that the Croats do not notice what is going on. They try to reduce Croatian patriotism to a "private matter" of a barbeque and spritzers. To cram their religion into a cramped sacristy, to re-educate their identity, and to compress their lively, active and creative Croatian national spirit into four walls or send it abroad. That is Tito's recipe, which he took from the totalitarian Kingdom of Yugoslavia, and which the Kingdom, in turn, took from the principles of the ideologists of Greater Serbia.

The story about the increase in right-wing extremism and the Ustasha Movement is the fruit of the embodied and well-paid creative lie among us, the tactics of us or them, and of the desire to "be chasing up each other again". It is time that Croatia stops tacitly agreeing to supply the food chain of anti-Croatian extremists and their ideologists. It is time we seriously understood the warning of the SOA [Security and Intelligence Agency]. Its findings are confirmed in the Committee and the Bulletin synergy of messages. They both are, actually, food for the leftist and Chetnik extremism in the modern state of Croatia, which was established with the will of the Croatian people to have their own state, but also as the reaction to the leftist Yugo-communist and Greater Serbian Chetnik extremism, which at convenient moments turns into open anti-Croatian terror.

(hkv.hr 13 March 2017)

A century of Serbian terror 1918 - 2018

Only the SPC and Serbia do not recognize Stepinac's sainthood

By establishing a mixed Commission of the Church in Croatia and the Serbian Orthodox Church [SPC- *Srpska pravoslavna crkva*] on the Matter of the Canonization of Alojzije Stepinac, Pope Francis showed an unprecedented degree of "inclusiveness". If we use the jargon of political correctness, which was introduced into the public discourse by Prof. Plenković Jr, the Pope's Commission did not bring "political stability". That is, the Commission is not political arbitration or "polit-prostitution". The Commission based its work on previously defined rules, which did not allow an exit "through the chimney" (kjv) outside the documented truth.

Perhaps this is why there are no relevant statements by Croatian politicians after the Commission completed its work except for the inclusive Pupovac. It would be interesting, for example, to hear the opinion of the Government Vice-President Štromar, but also of others, especially the great "plebeians" and opportunist "demo-Christians". Only Milorad Pupovac, duty arbiter, was heard arguing in tearful voice as the spokesman of not only the meagre few thousands who voted for him, but also of Croatian political elites, as well as of the SPC and Serbia.

Therefore, there is no common standpoint even after the work of the joint Commission. Serbia is not interested in truth, they know who is right, as Serbian academician Matija Bećković nicely summarized it. The Party's interpretation of history continues to be right. Aleksandar Raković, a Serbian "historian", said that Serbia and the SPC "will not accept now, or in the future" Stepinac's sainthood, because Serbs were killed by the regime of the Independent State of Croatia. Archbishop Stepinac, however, was not part of Pavelić's regime. Instead, Stepinac was critical of all regimes in which he acted, whether it was the Greater Serbian regime of monarchist Yugoslavia, Pavelić's regime in the NDH or the totalitarian Yugo-communist regime of Marshal Tito.

The Greater Serbs and the communists have a problem with Stepinac from the moment he refused Tito's plan for the separation of the Church in Croatia from the pope and the Vatican. We can agree with the contesters of Stepinac' sainthood only on one point. Stepinac would not have been debatable to the SPC, Serbia, Tito and the Party and their followers at the time, had he accepted Tito's proposal on the separation of the Church from the pope and the Vatican. The SPC and KPJ/SKJ would have proclaimed him a saint even during his life, that is, a national hero, and would have ordained him with the highest Saint Sava and state decorations, and would have honoured him with honorary JAZU membership, possibly even SANU, and he would have had Džamonja's monument in Belgrade instead of Blažević's staged court case in Zagreb. Until May 1945, while they were in the forests lurking for power, they treated Archbishop Stepinac as a positive person. However, as soon as they conquered power by revolutionary methods, Stepinac became the subject of their assemblage. Why? Because he did not agree to the coalition project between the communists and the Greater Serbs on the eradication of the historically confirmed identity of Croatian people. The identity on which the establishment of the free Croatian state was founded several decades later.

Today Croatia does not have a common standpoint with Serbia on anything that is important – be it language, history of literature, Greater Serbian aggression and its causes and consequences, victims, borders, except for one thing – Serbia's entry into the EU, which is of strategic interest for Croatia, although it is not clear whether it is of strategic interest for Serbia. In addition to Serbia, Stepinac's sainthood is also disputable to blind Serbian followers in Croatia who openly voice their views and justification of the anti-Croatian policies from the period of Greater Serbian totalitarianism of monarchist Yugoslavia and the period of totalitarian Yugo-communist totalitarianism of the red fascist Tito.

The myths and forgeries of the Party's interpretation of history are the key factor for murky water hunters. Stepinac was too big a catch for them. They had the opportunity they will never have again. The mixed Commission was not the latest but the last opportunity to put arguments instead of Party interpretations to *urbi et orbi*. The SPC representatives did not bring anything to the Commission! However, they asked for an extension of the Commission's work. They want to delay it forever. They will delay it no longer before the Pope but mostly in Croatia. The delaying will be successful as long as the internal plan for the Croatian state will allow it, that is, for as long as Croatian political elites continue to "include", feed, finance and boost those murky water hunters. While on the external plan they keep silence about the truth and the attacks on that truth.

When asked whether Stepinac was a controversial person Pupovac responds – there are still a number of questions that have to be answered. There is no approval on Stepinac, Pupovac explains, regarding his relationship with the NDH, the conversions, crimes.... Either he did not read the documents and other history material that have long been available, or he is manipulating, or he is a believer in the Party interpretations and montage.

It is utterly irrelevant to look at Cardinal Stepinac in relation to the Croatian-Serbian and Serbian-Croatian controversies after the end of the mixed Commission's work. The reason for the Pope to establish the mixed Commission was to contest Stepinac's sainthood. A contestation based on myths, lies, montages and forgeries is a Serb specialty, raised to the honour of state politics. Stepinac is a political issue for Serbia, for the Serbian Orthodox Church and their followers. For Catholics, the West and the Vatican, Stepinac is not a political issue. For Western civilization he is above all a lighthouse and a way finder to the proper stance towards totalitarianism. Regardless whether it is Greater Serbian, Ustasha or Yugo-communist. Therefore, if the Croatian state really wants to follow Stepinac's positive example, it must clearly, loudly, unambiguously and continuously condemn the Greater Serbian (1918-1941) and Communist (1945-1990) totalitarianism, the same way it condemns the Ustasha regime (1941-1945).

Serbia and the SPC alone in the world do not and will not officially recognize Alojzije Stepinac's sainthood. That is the sole tangible result of a year's work of the Pope's mixed Commission. Therefore, in regards to Stepinac - *santo subito*. And to continue the dialogue, not as a mute to a deaf person, but only and exclusively on the principles of international law, scientific apparatus and documented truth. All else is a waste of time, except when it comes to the necessary efforts to unmask the Greater Serbian and Communist myths, falsifications and forgeries.

(hkv.hr. 30 August 2017)

From Tokyo 1975 to Jasenovac 2017: a legitimate way of introducing anarchy

Velebit has been burning for seventeen (in numbers: 17) days in a row as I am writing this and looking for literature to revise the material on the cooperation of Italian fascists and Serbian Chetniks at the beginning of the forties of the past century. The de-stabilising of the State and the nation will last until September following the series of fires neatly announced in the fifth column newspaper *Novosti*. Pupovac and Radin announced this in joint comrade force and a certain Štromar joined them. The memorial plaque will have to be removed, wrote Milorad, Furio and Predrag in a message to Plenković. The boys knew that for Plenković the memorial monument in Jasenovac was far less important than political stability, that is, the "possibility to manage the state in a stable manner", as formulated by Gianni Agnelli, President of Fiat and one of the founders of the Trilateral Commission, in the introduction to the Italian edition of the report *Crisis of Democracy*, outlined at the Trilateral Meeting in Tokyo in 1975.

Because of political stability and a stable management of the Government, Plenković made Pupovac inclusive and gave him the golden calf position, and to Radin that of vice-president of Office for Ratification of European Directives, while Štromar, with his chronic lack of democratic legitimacy disorder, got the position from which he can lecture Croats and say what Plenković, as president of the "central national party" simply must not say without entering the "lack of democracy" zone. Now we are where we are. The political stability put together in the Plenković manner functioned only for one summer during which only the wild fires were stable.

The public does not know what was agreed on within the promiscuous coalition. However, it is known how real coalitions are con-trac-ted, which comes from the word "contract". Štromar, out of precaution, said that a "document was signed" without deadlines for carrying out what they have agreed to do, which means that they signed a paper without legitimate effect. A coalition contract, unless it is a partnership, must be public. On the other hand, coalitions are negotiated without a contract or with a "signed document" not made public, more-or-less on the territory of unified Yugoslav cultural territory of brotherhood and unity. If we are

A century of Serbian terror 1918 - 2018

to believe Plenković's inclusive group, it is agreed that the coalition of brotherhood and unity will devastate the monument to killed Croatian veterans in September this year.

To the task, comrades! The government was given the task by the inclusive representatives with the "lack of democracy" to do that "legally", that is, forcing the legal state, humiliating Croatian war veterans, chipping away at the foundation of the State, and falsifying historical facts. The memorial plaque, just as the Association HOS [Croatian Defense Forces], was placed according to all positive and valid regulations of the Republic of Croatia, however, it was not placed according to valid regulations of the Socialist Republic of Croatia, the Socialist Federative Republic of Yugoslavia and of the Republic Serbian Krajina. And only that is disputable.

The coalition agreement was obviously drawn in the spirit of and under the slogan "Death to fascism, freedom to the people". Hence, the silly question – should the monument to the killed Croatian veterans be dismantled or should it be the agreed coalition, that is, the Government founded on election fraud – if it dares destroy the monument to those who were killed in defense of the Homeland. Who knows what else they thought out while scheming to compose the coalition of brotherhood and unity and justifying it with arguments from Tokyo (1975)?

All this opens already known questions that are always swept under the rug again. For me personally the most interesting is the following: who and for whose benefit established the political system in Croatia in which three political models of state management are mixed by mutual agreement: the democratic, the monarchist and the oligarchist. I am just reading the book written by Domenico Moro (Profil, Zagreb, 2014), entitled *The Bilderberg Club and the Trilateral* with the profitable marketing subtitle *People who rule the world* and a rather failed message on the cover page: *Shocking discoveries about two secret societies of the most powerful people who decide about the fate of us all* (that is, there is nothing shocking, not even the discoveries of what was unknown). I thought that the book would offer at least an introduction to the answer, but I see that I must rely on common sense and only "acknowledge" the data in the book, in the same way in which our always brave and for the Homeland ready Zrinjevac [Ministry of Foreign Affairs and European

Integration in Zagreb] acknowledged the State Department's report on the situation of religious freedom in Croatia degraded to the level of the ethno-businessman's newspaper *Novosti*.

The thread that runs through the democratic, monarchist and oligharchist system in our country is red, the one that Jakov Blažević[32] sought. It is no secret that it survived thanks to the lack of lustration which the Croatian naïve politicians agreed upon thinking that the leopard changes its nature together with its spots. Therefore, as far as I have understood the mentioned book, the democratic system manifests itself in regular elections. After the election, the winners of the elections (party, local, state…) behave like monarchs. They are supported in that by the elites, who function, left and right, up and down, on state budget like an oligarchy in the service of a monarch. With this book, the author tries to enter the sociology of global elites, but in fact, more can be understood when the reader copies the presented facts into their own, so to speak - national - framework.

The author says that already several decades ago the Bilderberg and Trilateral representatives determined during their meetings that the "surplus of democracy" disturbs them. They resolved that surplus by decreasing parliamentary authority to the level of ratification, by increasing the powers of the executive authority and by the "affirmation of the unquestionable principle of the balanced and stable state management." Add to this also the introduction of "electoral laws that marginalize political forces beyond the area of 'moderate' political classification." Bearing in mind these observations, it is easier to understand our present-day despair, our Pupovacism, our Radinism and Štromarcism. They are the product of the "lack of democracy", of disastrous electoral legislature, the monarchist authority of mandatories, and partly of the outsmarting of democratic will. All of what was recommended in Tokyo in order to "manage the state in a stable way". However, it was forgotten that sometimes a stick has two ends.

---

32 Jakov Blažević, communist champion and chief prosecutor in the staged trial of Archbishop Alojzije Stepinac in 1946.

A century of Serbian terror 1918 - 2018

The memorial plaque in Jasenovac is not a question for the Republic of Croatia and its government. It is a question for the politicians of former and deceased SRH, SFRY and RSK. Why did the mandatory/monarch get into the situation in which Pupovacism, Radinism and Štromarcism can credibly blackmail him? For "political stability"? Or is the memorial plaque just a smoke screen, a search for reasons to escape from the current unsustainable situation of rotten "political stability"? Or else, is the plaque, unquestionable to a normal person, used to distract attention from the fact that the coalition was agreed only in order to "hibernate the summer."

Although the memorial plaque in Jasenovac was placed legitimately, if we are to believe the *Jutarnji List* newspaper, Plenković is looking for a legal way to destroy it. He will probably adopt a law on the legal destruction of the formerly legal memorial through a political decision to proclaim it illegal (on the tracks of exterminating the surplus of democracy), on the grounds that it irritates the brotherhood and unity of Pupovacism, Radinism and Štromarcism. And that law, whatever its name, can only and exclusively be pro-Yugoslav, that is, anti-Croatian. He allegedly said "we will find a legal way to exchange the plaque", which is the logic of an enforcer of the "shortage of democracy". On the same track, can he find a legal way to destroy the memorial in the town of Srb, which glorifies the Chetnik rebellion? Is the Chetnik rebellion legal? Why doesn't he find a legal way to abolish the Marshal Tito Street in Zaprešić, where the Mayor is his Party's presidency member, and the Minister of Internal Affairs is its citizen?

Because of its meaningless "strategic aims", the HDZ party was already paying extortion to hardcore Yugo-fans when it agreed to decrease the number of Croatian diaspora representatives to the level of the Serbian national minority, which was a betrayal of national interests justified by the "entry into the EU". That justification should not surprise us. In fact, as Moro wrote: "In Europe and in Italy all of that happened in the context of weakening the national state through the process of European unification. Exactly the way Crozier predicted it (in Tokyo in 1975, author's comment), European unity was a way of rejecting old ways of management, which favored the surplus of democracy and social demands that were very unpleasant for the transnational elite. After all, the topic of European unification was very frequent at the Bilderberg meetings, whose founder, Joseph Retinger, was inspired by the European Movement, the organisation that led to the establishment of the European Union." (p. 111)

Let's be honest, after the Party and Tito, our post-Tuđman elites have found new transnational masters. Therefore, many things which we know, and many more we don't yet know now well enough, are being refracted on the memorial to the killed Croatian veterans in Jasenovac. At this moment we know that transnational elites deeply-rooted in Pupovacism, Radinism and Štromarcism are against the memorial, under the slogan – let's not allow Croats a surplus of democracy. And that which we still don't know is for how long are we going to tolerate that at our expense they embitter our lives each day.

While I am finishing these notes Velebit, as I hear, continues burning and the wind turned to northern. Luckily I remember where I placed the primary literature about the cooperation, sorry – about the agreed coalition of Italian fascists and Serbian Chetniks in Croatia, so my next few days will be entertaining.

(hkv.hr, 29 August 2017)

The memorial plaque in Jasenovac: Coordination of Greater Serbian and Yugo-communist totalitarianism

In the twentieth century Croatia was confronted by three totalitarianisms. In the period from 1918 to 1941, the Greater Serbia Chetnik totalitarianism was destroying Croatia. The Ustasha movement was created as a reaction to that. In the period from 1941 to 1945, Croatia faced the Ustasha totalitarian regime. In the period 1945 to 1990, with the Yugoslav communist totalitarian regime, which experienced its renaissance in Croatia on 3 January 2000, and which continues to this day. Every totalitarianism is dangerous, especially the ones that lasted a long time. The best answer to all three totalitarianisms was the one given by Saint Alojzije Stepinac, the true ideal in relations towards totalitarian regimes.

A century of Serbian terror 1918 - 2018

The roots of the Greater Serbian Chetnik totalitarianism and the Yugoslav communist totalitarian regime reached deepest inside us, which could be clearly seen also this week in the context of the coordinated transfer of the memorial plaque to Croatian veterans of the Homeland war and precisely those who confronted these two totalitarianisms and founded the modern Croatian state. The state that is a pure negation of the goals of both the Chetnik Greater Serbian totalitarianism and the Yugoslav communist totalitarian regime.

During the twentieth century the Greater Serbian totalitarianism and Yugoslav communist totalitarian regimes, whether alone or in totalitarian coalition, lasted in Croatia a total of 68 (in numbers: sixty-eight) years. During the twentieth century the Ustasha totalitarian regime lasted from 10 April 1941 to 8 May 1945. A total of 49 months, that is 4.08 years. This data clearly illustrates that in Croatia there are many more hidden and visible Chetnik and communist snakes than Ustasha ones.

The remnants of these two long-lasting totalitarian regimes, joining together in both formal and informal coalition groups and units, produce fascism in Croatia in order to survive the circumstances of their negation in the democratic Republic of Croatia. To that end they first invent the lie that the Greater Serbian Chetnik totalitarianism and the Yugoslav communist totalitarian regime simply do not exist. They then invent the lie that only one totalitarianism (Ustasha/fascist) operates in Croatia, even though objectively it does not exist. Since it has not existed for a long time, Croatian war veterans become their "duty fascists", as well as all those who created the modern Republic of Croatia. The Croatian little Judas and the Yugoslav little Yudas are actually getting even with the democratic state in Croatia under the mask of dealing with Ustasha totalitarianism.

I drive almost every day by an elementary school which was recently nicely renovated. There is a tall obelisk at the entrance to the school yard. There is a biggish five-pointed red star planted on top of it, the star under which the aggressors entered occupied Vukovar. The elementary school is located just a few kilometers from the large uninvestigated tomb where victims of the red communist totalitarian five-pointed star were killed and thrown without sentence or evidence. The tomb has not been explored. I have not seen any obelisk with a horned letter U [Ustasha] in any school yard in Croatia because there is no such a thing. However, it is known that monuments are being built also to the Chetniks precisely with those symbols under which they rose up against the constitutional system of the democratic Republic of Croatia and committed a crime against peace and left behind, among other, more than 150 mass graves in Croatia. Just as the partisans did in 1945-46.

These two non-lustrated totalitarianisms are the context that removed the legitimately installed memorial plaque to Croatian war veterans in Jasenovac. It is a matter of violence, an illegal destruction not only of the monument raised to the killed and massacred Croatian heroes who were killed by the Greater Serbian and Yugo-communist totalitarianism in defense of the Homeland, but also of undermining the foundations of the state precisely by those who are guilty for the death and massacre of Croatian war veterans. The message is very clear: a fascist is a person who defends Croatia and the criterion is the theory and practice of Yugo-communism. Croatia is less Croatian in the smelly domains of the Greater Serbian and Yugo-communist myths engaged in the implementation of totalitarianism.

A government that does not understand this, cannot be Croatian. A government of Greater Serbian Chetnik totalitarianism and the Yugoslav communist totalitarian regime can only be totalitarian. While those Ready for the Homeland were losing their lives, the above totalitarianisms survived the "transition" and took advantage of it to grab privileged positions from which they could control the processes, the state and the people. They accepted the grace of abolition by the Croatian State, prevented legal and civilized social lustration from remnants and servants of the Yugo-communist regime, looted whatever could be looted, encumbered the state with debts, impoverished the people, destroyed villages, created relations that encourage ethnic cleansing of Croats from Croatia, and outside of any law, lustrated the democratic forces, living and past, ready to defend and build a home. With this they achieved the goals of both totalitarianisms: an ever-weaker Croatia, all the way to its new "annexation".

The reaction of the Croat people to the imposed unhealthy situation will happen regardless of the fact that both totalitarianisms have united and surrounded themselves by specialists in general national defense

A century of Serbian terror 1918 - 2018

and social self-protection of their brotherhood and unity. God forbid we wait too long! However, it is important to warn that those who will carry out the rehabilitation of the Croatian society will immediately be labeled as "fascists" and intertwined with infiltrated agents. Therefore, they must get well prepared on the theoretical plane and must reject right-wing romanticism from the start but undertake political realism (like Orban) on the lines of Starčević – Radić – Stepinac – Tuđman. Without a thorough analysis and clear synthesis, without the unity of local and diaspora Croatia, without clearly defined goals, the political fight (which undoubtedly lies ahead) for a democratic Croatia against the renewed totalitarianisms will be condemned to failure.

(hkv.hr. 8 September 2017)

For the Homeland: what is compromised in Croatia?

The representatives and servants of the rehabilitated Greater Serbian and Yugo-communist totalitarianism are competing these days in the search of an acceptable argument, or at least a phrase, with which they would additionally castrate Croatia, humiliate the Croats and their idea of an independent, democratic and sustainable state. For example, we have heard that the salute Ready for the Homeland is – "compromised". They probably consider that it is compromised by the four-year Ustasha regime. However, was that salute de-compromised in the eight-year Homeland war?

It was, of course, because the anti-fascist fighters used it against the coalition of Greater Serbian and Yugo-communist aggressors. What can be controversial when a Croatian anti-fascist who is Ready for the Homeland fights against any type of fascism, even the Greater Serbian and Yugo-communist fascism? To be ready for the homeland does not mean being a fascist, but exactly what it says – being ready for the homeland. The governing authorities are sending the message: you can be defenders who are Ready for the Homeland, but not in public, only between your four walls, or better still, on a long-term provisional job abroad.

From the Croatian side the problem appears in the Yugo-communist non-acceptance of the fact that the Homeland War is the foundation of the Croatian state. From the Greater Serbian side this problem is pathologically irrational. The Serbian Foreign Minister Ivica Dačić defined it at the beginning of September by saying that the stories about the Greater Serbian aggression on Croatia are a big lie. If there is no Greater Serbian aggression (fascism), there is no Homeland War (anti-fascist), if there is no aggression then there is no defense against it - instead there is a gratuitous "expulsion of Serbs". If the aggression is a lie then also the Homeland War is a big lie too. And so round and round.

A selective thesis about Croatia being compromised is now also incorporated into that construct. Its intention is that the Homeland War was – compromised, not just unnecessary. If it was compromised then the Croatian state is also permanently compromised, "always and forever" in one way or another. In the eyes of Greater Serbianism and Yugo-communism Croatia is uncompromised only if it does not exist, or if it is narrowed down to the degree that it does not have access to the sea.

From the viewpoint of the Croatian state, founded on the will of the Croatian people and the Homeland War of Independence there are, indeed, lots of things in Croatia that are compromised. All Governments in the past seventeen years are compromised because, with more or less passion, they carried out the thesis that the state does not rest on the will of the Croatian people and on the Homeland War. Including also this last Government. Had it accepted those two basic facts then the problem with the memorial plaque would not be a problem of the State or the Nation, but only a problem of Greater Serbian and Yugo-communist totalitarianism which must not in any form be part of the Croatian Government, especially not against electoral results.

From the same viewpoint regarding the foundation of the Croatian state, Croatia's budget is also compromised because it financed the reconstruction of the Greater Serbian and Yugo-communist totalitarianism. The Croatian Assembly is also compromised because it made decisions and passed laws that favoured the advocates and executors of theses on the Serbian aggression being a lie, and that defense from the aggression was "compromised". Presidents Mesić and Josipović are also compromised, but neither were prosecuted or revoked.

A century of Serbian terror 1918 - 2018

Whole parties are compromised. The SDP with their famous exit from the Assembly hall at a crucial moment for the State and the Nation, and the HDZ for the betrayal of Tuđman, Radić and Starčević. Cultural institutions on the state budget are also compromised. The media are also compromised. How many times was just the obscure *Novosti* newspaper compromised? The "public institution" in Jasenovac is also compromised as the prosthesis of the Greater Serbian myth moved into the twenty-first century. The entire European Council is also compromised, together with the EU that was compromised long ago, by not opposing France and Germany's current thesis on a multi-speed Europe with which the Croats had never and nowhere agreed.

Should it want to "turn to the future" Croatia must, due to ethics and logic, answer the question (to the guarantors of common sense) on who was compromised during the Greater Serbian and Yugo-communist aggression on Croatia. Yet instead of the answer, Croatian Judas and Yugoslav Yudas accept again the Greater Serbian and Yugo-communist thesis constructed on forgeries and myths. For example, the Serbian Party founded by the criminal Goran Hadžić is undoubtedly contaminated, however, in the state that was a victim of the aggression that Party is raised to the honour of immunity with a practical function of undisturbed arbitration throughout the whole political field. Allowing something like that borders with open high treason. From such a position the professional compromiser of the state and the nation gives lessons to Zagreb about the late Janko Bobetko, highest ranking general in the Croatian Army, by opposing the naming of a street after him.

From the viewpoint of the Croatian state, created with the will of the Croatian people as expressed in the referendum and the Homeland War, the de-Tuđmanisators are also compromised, but remained untainted even in the HDZ Party after the de-Tuđmanisation ideological fall. The systematic contamination and compromising of President Tuđman and of the Homeland War is the permanent politics of the Greater Serbian and Yugo-communist totalitarianism.

Can the Croatian Government clearly say who has contaminated the coexistence of Croatian Serbs with Croats? Is the Serbian Orthodox Church – SPC a permanently compromised Church before and during the aggression, or does the Catholic Church, whose symbol was Stepinac yesterday and Košić today, continue to be "compromised"? Is Pupovac permanently contaminated by the case of the false accusation of Croatia slaughtering eleven thousand Serbian children, or perhaps in the case of the tragic destiny of Dr. Ivan Šreter? Why is Pupovac de-compromised but Croatian patriotic veterans are compromised and expelled from Jasenovac? Who is it that wants to push the thesis that Croatian veterans are in fact Ustasha to an operational level? The fifth column. The Greater Serbs and Yugo-communists. Nobody else.

The correct question is: is Pupovac just a peacetime version of Goran Hadžić? If it is so then his inclusion into the government is a serious safety issue! However, if he is not a peacetime Goran Hadžić, what shall we do about the responsibility for the lie about the eleven thousand slaughtered Serbian children? Who and for what reason pardoned him in the name of the state and the people for such a primordial lie worthy of the Tartarus underworld that, at a special war level, ranks with the myth of the 700,000 Jasenovac victims? Is the aim of the illegal, but nevertheless bestowed, "absolution" the reconstruction of Yugoslav relationships in Croatia?

Over the past seventeen years in Croatia all that created, defended, succeeded in defending, liberated and achieved international recognition for the Croatian State has been compromised. At the same time, everything that did, does, or tries to oppose the Croatian State earned recognition. And if we consistently accepted the newest mantra about contamination, instead of special democratic elections, we would within a couple of months be able to establish all conditions for a civil war, and not just a verbal one. Because there is no country in the world that accepts the principle of contamination in order to reach its own negation, while at the same time feeding, abolishing, validating, privileging and heavily paying professional compromisers of the state and the nation. Actually, peacetime aggressors.

The Croats must take four steps in order to preserve their hard-won democratic and free State:

1. Remove the Greater Serbian and Yugo-communist totalitarianism from the government; 2. Establish a Croatian government accountable to the Croatian people; 3. Treat all totalitarianisms the same way: the

A century of Serbian terror 1918 - 2018

Greater Serbian, the Ustasha and the Yugo-communism; 4. Encourage, cultivate and achieve recognition for the values on which the Croatian identity is based, and at the same time investigate all the mass grave pits, starting with Jasenovac.

(hkv.hr, 12 September 2017)

Who is protecting Greater Serbian totalitarianism from facing the past?

Academician Zvonko Kusić, president of the "Committee for Confronting Consequences of Totalitarian Regimes" declared that "the task of the Committee is limited to the period from the beginning of World War II to the Homeland War". He skipped the period from 1918 to 1941, when Croatia was exposed to Greater Serbian totalitarianism. The basic EU documents mention the need to face the consequences of totalitarian, and not undemocratic regimes, since even a democratically elected government can behave undemocratically, but that still does not mean that it is a totalitarian regime. In addition, the European resolutions speak about the entire twentieth century, and not an abbreviated one. In the twentieth century, Croatia was devastated by three, and not by two, "undemocratic regimes".

To whom does it suit that the Committee does not discuss the entire twentieth century and all three totalitarianisms? Why did the official Croatia reduce this great European topic and the entire twentieth century only to the period from the beginning of World War II to the beginning of the Homeland War? Did it not thereby render impossible for the state and the nation to face the consequences of Greater Serbian totalitarianism? It is a case of a truncated period; hence the conclusions of the Committee will necessarily also be truncated. Incomplete.

The shortening of the last century exempted the Greater Serbian totalitarian/undemocratic regime from facing consequences. And a space was opened for its undisturbed rehabilitation and renewal. The Greater Serbian undemocratic regime is crucial to the understanding of the other two "undemocratic regimes", the Ustasha and the Yugo-communist regimes. They did not fall out of the sky, but have their origin precisely in the Greater Serbian totalitarian regime. The first one opposed the Greater Serbian totalitarianism, the other was in close cooperation with it.

Without facing the Greater Serbian totalitarian regime, it is impossible to comprehend the reason for the Ustasha Movement, consequently also the Ustasha "undemocratic" regime. It was, in fact, the reaction to the Greater Serbian totalitarian regime. It experienced one of its peaks with the assassination of Radić and his HSS Party members in the Belgrade Parliament. Extensive historical material exists on the Greater Serbian totalitarian regime. Undeniably, it existed and left behind tragic consequences for the Croatian people and the state and we have to confront the consequences.

Without facing the Greater Serbian totalitarian regime, it is also impossible to understand the Yugo-communist "undemocratic" regime. The copy and paste method is exactly how Marshal Tito and his totalitarian KPJ/SKH applied the Old-Yugoslav Greater Serbian totalitarian approach towards Croats: Bleiburg, mass executions, political assassinations, emigration, economic drain, theft of territories, like-mindedness, censorship… A repetition of the subject matter with some new totalitarian innovations.

It is also difficult to understand the foundations of the modern Croatian state without facing the consequences of the Greater Serbian totalitarian regime from the first half of the 20th century. The Homeland War is the foundation of the Croatian state because it broke up with totalitarianisms and established a democratic state. It was the reaction to the Greater Serbian and Yugo-communist totalitarianism that acted in synergy ever since the mass changeover of the Chetniks to partisans, all the way to their joint aggression on Croatia in 1991. There are too many reasons that speak about the need to face the Greater Serbian totalitarianism. It would be good to hear the arguments on why this was bypassed.

The characteristics of Greater Serbian totalitarianism could vividly be seen in the occupied Croatian regions: ethnic cleansing, mass burial pits, general plunder, culturecide, urbicide, memorycide, Vukovar, Škabrnja... However, the Committee will not discuss that period either, although the aggression and the Greater Serbian regime that was established in the occupied regions belong to the twentieth century. They will discuss only the time "up to the Homeland War". With this, the Committee has thrown out from the twentieth century a complete and an incredibly brutal totalitarianism marked with serious crimes. Given the increase in Chetnik and Greater Serbian extremism, which the relevant bodies are continuously warning about (to which the politicians do not react), it may be reasonable to suppose that if we do not face it and its consequences, this totalitarianism, once in favourable political circumstances, will turn savage again.

It would be regrettable that the "Committee for Confronting Consequences of Totalitarian Regimes" turns into a defender of the Greater Serbian "undemocratic regime". In the current state of affairs, the Greater Serbian totalitarian undemocratic regime in Croatia is exempted, even partly privileged by somebody's political decision. Probably until it recovers from "historic" defeats in the Homeland War, and encouraged by the Croatian lack of facing its criminal consequences, it attempts once again to establish its "undemocratic" regime in Croatia. Who, where and when made the political decision to abolish a totalitarianism?

The Homeland Security Council and even the SOA [Security and Intelligence Agency], should warn the Committee for Confronting Consequences of Totalitarian Regimes about the arguments and importance of treating and endorsing the Greater Serbian totalitarianism in the same way as the other two "undemocratic regimes".

(hkv.hr, 15 September 2017)

Croatian strategic interest: monument to Tepić as ticket for Serbia's entry to the EU

Serbia raised a monument to terrorist Tepić[33]. Croatia defeated the aggressor's various 'Tepićs' and 'Captain Dragans' in the war that was inflicted upon it. It then allowed that a minister in the Serbian Republic of Krajina, the aggressor's formation on Croatian territory, became president of a Croatian political party and a parliamentary representative. That was a clear message to the aggressor state to continue with the peacetime aggression. And continue it did, not only with raising monuments to its terrorists, but now even by wanting to prescribe laws to the Croatian State, which former Prime Minister Milanović called an "accidental State". Monuments are also accidentaly raised and aggressions glorified in Croatia, such as the one of 1941, and the one of 1991. The conditions for a new aggression are therefore being created.

Croatia now heavily finances the Belgrade branch in Croatia. It pays for the anti-Croatian *Novosti* newspaper, it holds Pupovac like the apple of its eye, laws are passed in his favour, even constitutional laws. Also, the Croatian judiciary' sentence allowed terrorist Dragan Vasiljković to freedom. What an idyll for the aggressors! Croatia only needs to be disarmed and there we are, at the beginning of the end, and the end of the beginning.

Besides, Croatian politicians do not mention at all the Greater Serbian regime of monarchist Yugoslavia, the Serbian Nazi regime in World War II and the slaughter of Jews – more successful than that in the Independent State of Croatia (NDH), nor the two aggressions committed on Croatia. Only Minister Tomo Medved and parliamentary representative Miro Kovač voiced their views regarding the monument to Tepić, which represents next to nothing in Tuđman's [HDZ] Party. The

---

33 Milan Tepić, major in the Yugoslav People's Army, commander of the Barutana Depot in Bedenik near Bjelovar, refused to surrender to Croatian forces on 29. 09. 1991 by blowing up an arms store and killing 11 Croatian fighters. On 29. 09. 2017, a monument to Major Tepić was unveiled in Belgrade, near to a street that bears his name, with high representatives of the Serbian Government conducting the ceremony and labelling his suicidal act as 'heroic'.

A century of Serbian terror 1918 - 2018

inclusive opposition in the government did not say a word on the matter, and neither did the as yet non-inclusive opposition within the mandatory's authority.

The privileged Belgrade agents are not hiding anymore as the Labradors[34] did earlier. Since Plenković, in the manner of a forceful monarch, imposed the inclusive government, order, regime and system of values, the Belgrade agents swiftly swung into action to create internal relationships befitting forces that were defeated in the Homeland War. Education and family are among the victims of the inclusive government in Croatia, as are some of the ministers who received the monarch's public rebuke with elements of trampling on human dignity (Barišić, Tolušić, Murganić...).

Štromar, Pupovac and Radin became the untouchable three kings of the promiscuous inclusive politics. All three did not achieve the number of votes of an average representative. What is their view on the fact that Serbia is raising monuments to people who conducted the Greater Serbian aggression on Croatia? Silence. No comment. And they sit in the executive and legislative government! *Sapienti sat.*

Due to their attitude towards the foundations of the Croatian state among other, the inclusive factors who are a burden on the Croatian hump, obtained lean democratic legitimacy in the elections. However, the lower their democratic legitimacy, the bigger their chances for inclusivist trafficking. It must be acknowledged that inclusivist trafficking in Croatian politics was splendidly introduced by the current mandatary, Plenković Jr., the defender of "political stability". In strong monarchist manner, just like Sanader installed Pupovac "forever" in the position of Belgrade governor of Croatia.

He left the education to Štromar's cronies. The internal politics and manufacture of Ustasha to Pupovac's lot. Radin's comrades got the Assembly above which there is only the monarch. He left the function of monarch and foreign policy spokesman to himself, because only that way

---

34 Anti-Croatian subversive terrorist groups of the Counter-intelligence Service (KOS) of the Yugoslav People's Army that operated in 1991 under the name Labrador.

can he more or less play the role of a political figure at home and abroad. Since the inclusive government and the entire inclusive array do not have an official view about the fact that the aggressor is raising monuments to glorify the aggression on Croatia, then the legitimate question is: to what extent is that a Croatian government, especially in view of the fact that at the same time it is moving legal and lawful monuments to Croatian fighters in Croatia who chased away the Tepićs and Captain Dragans. A government is Croatian to the degree in which it reflects the democratically expressed will of the Croatian people. And in our case, that is – God save us! Zero points.

However, at the moment only blogger Ivica[35] is bringing down the inclusive retinue, who previously financially successfully brought down Agrokor – who knows on whose account and whose order. The opposition does not bring down the inclusives (except for Bernardić's folk performances), because they conduct its politics even better than the SDP's sixth worst government in the world according to the World Economic Forum criteria.

Since there is no position or opposition, it is time, therefore, that people take matters into their own hands and start making decisions about their own fate. The inclusive government is unable to recognise even the basis on which Croatian dignity must be defended in the people's name, as seen in the silence regarding the monument to Tepić. The Štromar's, Pupovac's and Radin's minorities, or the - until recently - privileged blogger Ivica, are even less capable to give this serious consideration. They all fell out of the same sack in fact, in which Croatia is seen as a milking cow. An object for milking. And not a subject with its own dignity.

While finishing this little text in agricultural tone, I ask myself whether the often emphasized, but never democratically verified, official

---

35 Ivica Todorić, head of Agrokor, the largest private company in Croatia, which made illegal profits and misused trust in economic affairs for a number of years until in 2018 it went into administration, with prosecution and scandal enveloping many public figures in government, banking, industry and devastating consequences for large and small companies with the loss of many jobs.

 A century of Serbian terror 1918 - 2018

standpoint is still actual regarding Serbia's entry into the European Union being in the Croatian strategic interest. It is [actual] with the monuments to Tepić and Draža, of course. I muse on Croatia being a member of the EU but sporting a mausoleum to the war criminal Šoškoćanin and the Chetnik uprising in the town of Srb! Parallel with the reality of the Croatian nation taking place in their state, the Yugoslav reality is also taking place within it.

Or does the Croatian state have some conditions towards Serbia relative to borders, war compensation and the de-fascistisation of Serbia? If they exist, could the mandatary-monarch and his three democratically anorexic kings define them, explain them, publicly say and stand by them? If they don't exist, then as citizens, we must accept domestic milking. And we shall continue to do so until we kick so fiercely that we throw the milking team as far as possible from our beautiful little stable and its decision-making places.

The monument to Tepić is a pledge for future Serbian aggressions. As it was already announced –Serbia will "by all available means" prevent future Croatian liberating actions, which cannot be implemented without the inclusivist politics within Croatia. The milking team does not see any problem with that, and that is the key problem for Croatia today.

(hkv.hr, 1 October 2017)

The problems of avoiding two lustration laws

Croatia missed the opportunity to enter the essence of democratic society due to, among other things, failing to pass two lustration laws, and due to passing a large number of laws and loopholes in the law, which are harmful to the state and the nation. Today it is obvious even to incorrigible sceptics that it was necessary to pass a law on the lustration of communist remnants. And it was also necessary to pass a law on the lustration of Greater Serbian remnants.

The first law succeeded to reach the Croatian National Assembly twice, on the proposal of the Croatian Party of Rights [HSP], but it was successfully dismissed on the proposal of the Croatian Democratic Union. Instead, according to law founded on European standards, there followed the non-democratic persecution of Croatian veterans, the de-Tuđmanization and the Lex Perković[36]. In a word, proletiariat dictatorship, as the communists would origninally call it. The HSP was pushed out of the National Assembly.

The second indispensable lustration law regarding Greater Serbian remnants in the Croatian society did not even succeed to reach the Croatian National Assembly, let alone the Croatian Assembly[37], nor was it, as far as I know, proposed by any Party. Instead, Croatia has shown exceptional grace with the masochistic law on the abolition of those destroying the State's constitutional position (*de facto* – terrorists!), and in passing laws that helped, for example, the SDSS party, founded by the Greater Serbian war criminal, to became a key factor in the survival of the Croatian Government and the main arbitrator of internal political activity.

The failure of political parties and their instant elites to pass the necessary laws and their passing of unnecessary ones, has brought the Croatian state to the very edge of its survival because the legislative politics established conditions for the rehabilitation of the two totalitarianisms which, partly separately and partly in strategic partnership, ruled Croatia for 70 years during the twentieth century. Between 1918 and 1941 and from 1945 to 1990 or 1998, when the process of peaceful reintegration of the Croatian Podunavlje was completed. In the twentieth century, Croatia was not fully under the Greater Serbian and Yugo-communist totalitarian regime during the period 1900 and 1918, and from the end of the peaceful

---

36 *Lex Perković* – the law passed by Zoran Milanović's government in 2013, which involved constitutional changes and legal 'acrobatics' to bypass the European Arrest Warrant (EUN) and prevent the extradition of previous members of the Yugoslav and Croatian Secret Services to Germany, where they had assassinated Croatian national Stjepan Đureković because of his patriotic activities. Croatia, as newly accepted EU member at the time, suffered enormous damage and sanctions such as the freezing of funds for its inclusion in the Schengen zone. "Lex Perković" was abolished in 2014 and the criminals extradited, tried and sentenced to life imprisonment.

37 *Hrvatski državni sabor* – Croatian National Assembly is the historical name officially in use from 1918 until 1942 and between 1997 and 2001, when constitutional changes re-named it as The Croatian Assembly (*Hrvatski sabor*).

A century of Serbian terror 1918 - 2018

reintegration until 3 January 2000, when the rehabilitation of the remnants of Greater Serbian and Yugo-communist totalitarianism began.

The consequences are terrifying. Croatia is at the bottom of the European Union according to all crucial relevant present and future indicators, while at the same time it is the "Western Balkans locomotive" from which local population is massively fleeing. The creation of such conditions in which a Croat in Croatia can no longer live in a dignified manner cannot be called Croatian politics because it is anti-Croatian.

The matter culminated with the rearrangement of election results in the latest state elections. The mandatary withdrew his original coalition partner and instead included in the government the party founded by the Greater Serbian war criminal and the leading de-Tuđmanisation party. With this the processes of failure to pass the necessary laws and of passing unnecessary laws reached their peak, assuming executive and legislative power.

One arm of the pincers that tear apart the democratic Croatia established in the Homeland War are composed of totalitarian guardians of communist revolutionary achievements – supposedly they have become liberal regardless of party affiliation, and the other arm sticks to Belgrade politics on the Virovitica – Karlovac – Karlobag line. Both arms mask themselves as "antifascist" turning Croatia into a great carnival.

The first arm of the pincers is making a fool of the Croatian people by pick-pocketing them and stealing their future. The other arm is preparing the conditions for a new aggression with "all available means". The exit from the grip on Croatia will be painful for both restored totalitarianisms. When it happens, the story about reconciling the irreconcilable, the platitude about the need to forget the past, the stupidity about the need for inclusiveness for the sake of stability, will no longer 'hold water', just like the abolition of terrorists and non-lustration of ideologists and servants of the remnants of Yugo-communist and Greater Serbian totalitarianism.

Only then will Croatia become, on the internal level, a state in the full sense of the word. Until then we are to suffer and create conditions for another democratic movement of the Croatian people, which will help us rise to our feet from the present position – head down, hands on the back. It is important to recognize that we are again facing sophisticated forms of two totalitarianisms, which in synergy are becoming tougher.

In view of this, should it come to the announced referendum regarding changes to anti-Croatian electoral legislation, adapted to restoring the above mentioned two totalitarian remnants, we have to support it with all our heart, mind and soul. With our heart, because as long as there is heart, there will be a Croatia. With our mind, because without it, the heart cannot change anything in the objective world. And with our soul, because only with our own strength and God's help can we make Croatia Croatian. We have irresponsibly dropped all other tools from our hands.

(hkv.hr, 3 October 2017)

Several states in one Yugoslav society

The authors of the "European Vučić", are, in fact, "fascinated by the frivolous belief in the unstoppable progress" of the Western Balkans. What progress can be expected when a Chetnik is placed on the European pedestal? A backwards progress. Or a continuation of the circular course of history of Serbian frameworks in the territory of South-eastern Europe. This means that the creators of such platitude "are steeped in prejudices, superstition and ignorance, blinded with empty, intrusive visions of a utopian future, they reflexively suffocate every different opinion".

The agreement on normalisation of relations or strengthening regional cooperation?!

Many people were surprised by the invitation of the President of the Republic of Croatia addressed to the Serbian President to pay an official visit to Croatia, which Vučić immediately publicly accepted. The speed of the agreed meeting points to the conclusion that the visit was either previously agreed, or it happened at the command of more powerful players than the two Presidents. The arrows directed at President Grabar-Kitarović for inviting Vučić foresee several important details, which probably govern her decisions. But, the devil hides in the details.

Let's suppose that the Western Balkans bosses decided that now is the right moment for Vučić to visit Croatia. The people's pulse says quite the opposite, and the President knows it for sure. Nevertheless, she decides to invite Vučić, which directly challenges her second term of office. Perhaps there is something much more significant than the second term of office. What could it be?

It is perfectly clear that on a personal level, even after the visit to Zagreb, Vučić will remain the shaved Chetnik who participated in the aggression on Croatia. In the end, the problem is not about him, Croatia solved the Chetnik issue forever in 1995. It is not a question of saving Chetnik Vučić, but possibly saving the Western Balkans project and Belgrade as its central point. The project by Great Britain and the European Union indicates increasing weakness and its own unsustainability. It resolves nothing and makes problems more complex.

It is known that Croats are loyal to their partners, allies. The President has shown loyalty to the Western Balkans with the Vučić invitation. She could have at short notice invited, for example, Orban. However, she did not. Should we blame her for that? Yes and no. She neither established the Western Balkans, nor did she incorporate their destruction into her programme. She fulfills the obligations that her predecessors accepted as an integral part of the state foreign politics. And that has long been unsovereign and pro-Western Balkan.

In 1996, before accepting the Western Balkans strategies, when Croatia concluded the Agreement with SR Yugoslavia on the Normalisation of Relations between the Republic of Croatia and the

Federative Republic of Yugoslavia (it was signed by Mate Granić and Milan Milutinović) and confirmed by the House of Representatives of the Croatian National Assembly on 20 September 1996, few people believed that it would remain just on paper and would soon be replaced by the Western Balkans fog with corresponding strategy. The Agreement brought to the fore all the open issues between Zagreb and Belgrade. With that Agreement Belgrade admitted the defeat of Greater Serbian politics and the aggression on Croatia.

According to the Agreement it was necessary, without delay, to accelerate the process of resolving the missing persons issue; to declare absolution for acts committed in relation to armed conflicts, though excluding the most serious violations of human rights (war crimes); agreement was reached on mutual respect of sovereignty, territorial integrity and independence according to international law; on ensuring the conditions for free and safe return of refugees and displaced persons; and that within half a year, and this is important and crucial – the agreement will be reached regarding compensation for all destroyed, damaged and missing property. Serbia is the successor of the Federative Republic of Yugoslavia. Twenty-two years have passed since the Agreement was signed.

None of the Presidents of the Republic of Croatia did anything regarding an agreement on property compensation. Should this agreement be signed, or at least initiated, during the meeting of President Grabar-Kitarović and Vučić, then the President of the Republic will distantiate herself from the disastrous politics of Presidents Mesić and Josipović. However, if that agreement is not even mentioned, then it is clear that Kolinda Grabar-Kitarović is also governed by the same Western Balkans principles as her two predecessors.

The issue of war compensation is not a Western Balkans issue, but one of Croatian national interest. The official estimate of a competent state Commission on the amount of war compensation formerly arrived to 37,119,679,000 USD. This is a topic in which Serbia should also be interested, since its entry into the European Union cannot be supported by official Croatia without resolving the issue of war compensation, bar committing high treason. It is not a question of blackmailing Serbia. It is an issue of war compensation caused by the Greater Serbian aggression, which Belgrade admitted when it signed the Agreement in 1996. Serbia cannot send such an invoice to Croatia, because the war took place on the internationally recognized territory of the Republic of Croatia. Payment of war compensation leads to the normalization and mutual trust between the two states. Non-payment leads to the repetition of historical delusions on both the Serbian and Croatian side.

The second priority issue in the Agreement refers to the respect of sovereignty and territorial integrity. Serbia does not respect the Agreement, that is, Croatian sovereignty and territorial integrity, since it seized the river islets of Vukovar and Šarengrad, the areas of Kenđija and Karapandž…, which may be seen as not giving up on its territorial pretensions over Croatian territory. It is therefore a question of the State border. What will the President's meeting with Vučić bring in that regard? Should it bring nothing, the invitation and the meeting will represent a hiding to nothing from the standpoint of Croatian common sense. However, it is possible that from the standpoint of Western Balkans strategy implementation it may bring some fruits and benefit the WB strategists.

It is possible that Vučić promises to return several stolen objects of art, offers information about two-three missing Croatian persons in Serbian concentration camps, in order to avoid the discussion about the essence of the matter – the borders and war compensation. That way, the Western Balkan (neo-Yugoslav) manner of solving open issues would continue. If the Croatian President wants to justify her invitation to Vučić, she must put on the table the updating of the Agreement on Normalization. Point by point, article by article. Everything else is, from the standpoint of Croatian national interests, a trifle.

The 1996 Agreement represents the only solid foundation for Croatia and Serbia to strengthen mutual trust and tolerance in the issues of peace, stability and development in the region, as it is written in the Agreement. The meeting with Vučić must also be built on that Agreement. Not on Pupovac's provocations, Serbian exhibitions, statements about the "Ustasha's vicar" and similar dead-end tracks. Can the President rise to that level, or will she remain on Mesić's and Josipović's frog-level perspective?

Regarding the question of those Western Balkanic trifles on which Mesić and Josipović built the relations with Serbia, we must recall

A century of Serbian terror 1918 - 2018

the development of the Western Balkans strategy in Croatia that was implemented without exception by all democratically legitimate figures, starting with Račan and Mesić. In contrast to the 1996 Agreement on Normalization of Relations, there is a whole sequence of documents and initiatives, an entire Western Balkans machinery with the corresponding industry for production of consent. The President must decide whether she wants to serve the Agreement or the Western Balkans fogs.

During the conference of the Croatian Cultural Council at the end of 2009, Zdravka Bušić, the current State Secretary in the Ministry of Foreign Affairs, presented a detailed chronology of the West Balkans strategies. Let's follow its order: the Western Balkans is not an invention of populists, Eurosceptics or Europhobes, but a "serious international community project recorded in numerous documents, which is already being realized through very concrete projects in which Croatia has been participating for a long time". Croatia and Serbia are part of that WB project. Hence my fear, that the invitation and meeting with Vučić might be on the track of that international community's project, that is, instead of the normalization of relations, it is the "regional issues" that will actually be considered in their discussions.

And now Zdravka Bušić [points out]: "If you look at the European Union internet pages, you can see that from 1998 to this day many documents are entitled "Western Balkans" and in those documents the states are reduced to mere sub-regions of those Western Balkans. And while the official authorities try to conceal at any price the signs that would indicate the new Balkans community, the official European Union documents and the development of events prove that the Western Balkans strategy is already being successfully realized".

• In April 1997 the European Union General Council adopted the Policy of Regional Admission for the entry of Western Balkans countries (the term means the States of former Yugoslavia without Slovenia, and with Albania). The emphasis is on a collective admission.

• In March 1999, the European Commission wants to stabilize the entire Balkans region with the Process of Stabilisation and Association, which we know well.

• The Process of Stabilisation and Association of the countries or Southeastern Europe of May 1999 deals exclusively with regional admission and the "common strategy".

• The European Union in all its reports determines exactly the countries of the Western Balkans, and in the political sense, the Western Balkans represent a strictly determined foreign politics of the Union towards those countries, or "regional concept for the Western Balkans countries".

• The SECI was established as a specific association of Southeastern European countries, which was transformed into the Pact for Stability of Southeastern Europe, in order for the SEECP, the Process of Cooperation in Southeastern Europe, to later assume the functions of the Pact for Stability.

• Within the framework of the Council of Ministers of the European Union, a special regional Commission of the Council of Ministers for the Western Balkans was established. They meet regularly and publish documents about the Western Balkans, as a whole.

• The European Commission publishes annual reports on the achieved macro-economic and structural development of the "region" (we know that very well, because we always eagerly expect these reports to see if we obtained a passing grade).

• In November 2000, the European Union Western Balkanic Summit was held in Zagreb. It was renamed the "Zagreb Head Summit" in order to mitigate the tension which the term Western Balkanic provokes. The Final Report states: "From now on the Heads of State and Governments of the five States (Albania, Macedonia, Bosnia and Herzegovina, Croatia and Yugoslavia) (…) commit to reach agreements among their States about regional cooperation that foresee political dialogue, regional area of free trade" and other.

• Starting from those commitments, the President of the Republic Mesić and later Premier Sanader expressed many times that "Croatia will not flee the region". If we carefully trace back their activities, it is obvious that they loyally and diligently carried out the goals that were set.

• At the end of April 2001, Brussels "designed" an Agreement on Stabilisation and Association for the Western Balkans states. One year later the Initiative of European Stability (ESI) was established, as an independent and non-profit research and political institute, which will analyze more thoroughly the political issues related to Southeastern Europe.

• In 2003, the then Premier Ivo Sanader continued the politics of uniting the region and further strengthened it by creating the parliamentary "Alliance for Europe".

•Sanader's government crowned "regional cooperation" with the establishment of the Western Balkans zone of free trade, under the name of New CEFTA (Mid European Region of Free Trade).

• In June 2003, the meeting of the Ministers of Foreign Affairs on the Process of Cooperation in South-eastern Europe (SEECP) was held in Sarajevo.

• Also, in June 2003 the Salonika Summit was held in Greece, where the European Union confirmed with a joint declaration a clear perspective of membership for Croatia, Bosnia and Herzegovina, Serbia and Montenegro, Macedonia and Albania, as defined by the UN Security Council Resolution, thus as a team. The Salonika Agenda for the Western Balkans was also accepted, the document in which the priority reform steps for joining the European Union are defined for the five countries from the Process of Stabilisation and Association (Croatia, Bosnia and Herzegovina, Serbia and Montenegro, Macedonia and Albania).

• The European Council repeated its determination to fully and effectively support the European perspective on the Western Balkans countries and it stated that "the Western Balkans countries will become an integral part of the European Union, once they satisfy the established criteria". The Western Balkans Communities programmes were presented, thereby setting the frames and legal basis for the participation of individuals or institutions from the Western Balkans countries in the Community programmes.

• Since 2007, the Western Balkans countries were given the opportunity to continue their involvement in joint projects, for example, in the areas such as the environment, energy and transportation, research work, culture, media and other. Regional cooperation was additionally strengthened with the establishment of a certain number of different centers within the region.

• By the end of December 2006, the government of Ivo Sanader signed in Bucharest the Western Balkans Agreement on free trade with Albania, Bosnia and Herzegovina, Macedonia, Moldavia, Montenegro, Serbia and the UN Civilian Administrator in Kosovo. The Agreement was presented as the New CEFTA (Mid European Region of Free Trade). However, there was always one goal in the background: the strengthening of the assigned regional cooperation. These are only the key documents and the sequence of events that clearly illustrate the development of the Western Balkans strategy" – Zdravka Bušić said that at the Croatian Cultural Council conference in 2009.

Without going deeper into the probable motives and reasons that led to the invitation to Vučić and his hasty acceptance, it can be concluded that Vučić is very keen on attending the meeting. His motives are Western Balkanic, his tailwind comes from A. Merkel. The President's motives will be seen in the fruits of the meeting. The invitation undoubtedly exposed the President to landing on ice without skates. Only concrete results based on the 1996 Agreement can save her from a fall on domestic soil. They will be difficult to realize. Firstly, because Vučić is not interested in the implementation of the Agreement on Normalization, and secondly, because the pinning down of the issue is handled by the government, which, apparently was not included in the decision on inviting the Serbian President.

Finally, it is necessary to convey the partially quoted historical reminder. In Point 3 of the Final Declaration of the Western Balkans Summit (Zagreb, November 2000), the orders for the Western Balkans legitimacies are stated, which the President of the Republic must also respect to some extent: "From now on, Heads of State and Governments of the five States (Albania, Macedonia, Bosnia and Herzegovina, Croatia and Yugoslavia) that the process refers to, are obliged to reach agreements among their States about regional cooperation which foresee a political dialogue, a regional free trade area, as well as close cooperation in the area of the judiciary and internal affairs, especially in view of strengthening the court system and its independence, the fight against organized crime, corruption, money laundering, illegal immigration, slave trade and all other forms of smuggling. These agreements will be incorporated in the Agreements on Stabilisation and Association as they are achieved with the European Union. The Heads of State and Governments of the five countries mentioned have emphasized the importance they gave to the training of policemen, judges and the strengthening of border controls". It is quite possible that the Western Balkans Declaration has buried the 1996 Agreement, which also explains why it has not been implemented to this day.

The crucial question therefore concerns the fundamental approach to relations between Croatia and Serbia. Is that approach part of the Western Balkans "draughty" strategy, or is it an integral part of a realistic implementation policy of the Agreement on Normalization of Relations between the Republic of Croatia and the Federal Republic of Yugoslavia. In its relations with Serbia, it is certainly better for Croatia to insist on the signed Agreement. It is a bilateral issue between two sovereign states, not a Western Balkans issue. The Western Balkans, just as the Eastern Balkans, do not in fact exist in the objective world. However, Croatia and Serbia do exist and it is better for both states to exit the fog and settle their relations according to the principles concluded in their Agreement. Furthermore, it is an open issue on how much the 1966 Agreement fits into the phantom strategy of the Western Balkans at all, and vice versa.

The President of the Republic is on a more serious test than it may seem at first sight. Oh, yes, I forgot to praise Pupovac. He is quite right when he says that it is unreasonable to ask Vučić to apologize (a trifle). It is reasonable to ask Serbia to pay war compensation.

(hkv.hr, 2 February 2018)

The feast day of Stepinac in the atmosphere of Aleksandar Vučić's arrival

In June 2015 when Aleksandar Vučić, Serbian head of Government, current President of Serbia, tried to defend his minister's Aleksandar Vulin's statement in Jadovno about the "Ustasha vicar", he said "if you are trying to promote Alojzije Stepinac as a saint in Serbia or among the Serbs, that propaganda will not work". That was his contribution to the normalization of relations, entirely along the lines of the usual policy of the Serbian Orthodox Church and of Serbia. At the time he could not have dreamt that just before Stepinčevo in 2018, he would get an official invitation to visit Croatia, which took place only two days after the feast day by which Catholics commemorate the life, death and resurrection of the beatified and future saint Alojzije Stepinac. The model of relations towards all the totalitarianisms that he confronted.

In explaining the reason for inviting Vučić, President Kolinda Grabar-Kitarović said, among other things, that she wanted to avoid the escalation of the "verbal war". Lately it has not been a matter of a verbal war, but of a verbal (and active) Serbian foreign policy aggression on Croatia. At least two sides are necessary to define a war. Any defense from the aggression on legislative, executive, judicial and presidential levels is missing on the Croatian side. Therefore, there is no war.

Vučić's arrival in Zagreb throws a dark shadow on Stepinac' feast day. If his arrival was planned ahead, then it was not well planned. If the meeting was forced, it should have been postponed at least to the end of February. Most Croats' pulse beats with Stepinac's heart. It is not reasonable to bring the representative of the main negator of Stepinac's sainthood to Croatia on Stepinac' feast day. Regarding Stepinac, Serbia and the Serbian Orthodox Church, with their negative myth about Stepinac, cause heart arrhythmia in Croats. Since long ago. For decades. For example, even before World War II, when they tried to prevent the concordat with the Vatican, and when they were promoters and carriers of antisemitism in monarchist Yugoslavia. It seems that the regime in Croatia has collectively "forgotten the past and turned to the future" on their "path to Europe", which is rewritten into the Western Balkans strategy. Therefore, it is no longer able to react rationally even against a historically proven enemy.

During World War II, Serbia and the Serbian Orthodox Church gave an enthusiastic welcome to German authorities, praising Hitler and his system, bowing to him in hope that he would give them Great Serbia. They told Hitler that Croatia was not implementing the anti-Semitic policies to a satisfying degree. Serbia, however, with the persuasion and blessing of the Serbian Orthodox Church, thoroughly persecuted, humiliated, plundered and liquidated the Jews. The Serbian regime established four camps for that purpose in the area of Belgrade alone. In those camps, they systematically killed Jews, from pregnant women, mothers with infant children to the elderly. Before that, Serbian propaganda deprived Jews of humanity, the same way as the regime's man Frljić is depriving Croats of humanity today, just because they are Croats. The Serbian patent is also known, a bullet-proof station wagon – gas chamber.

On the eve and during World War II Stepinac was actively helping the Jews in Croatia. And also the Serbs who were endangered by the Ustasha regime during the war. Already then, the Serbian Orthodox Church and Serbia denounced him "Ustasha vicar" and criminal, disregarding their own participation in the holocaust. Greater Serbian politics and tactics are exactly the same in war and in peacetime conditions, in totalitarian Yugoslav or in democratic circumstances. However, the Croatian regime is still under the influence of Yugoslav brotherhood and unity in the Greater Serbian manner. Inasmuch it is less Croatian.

Even today, Serbia is building its foreign politics toward Croatia on the strengthening of the myth of Jasenovac, on the denial of Stepinac's sainthood and historical role, on the substitution of theses, on the promotion of anti-Croatian lies and the instrumentalisation of the Serbian national minority in Croatia. The first and the basic thesis of Serbian relations towards Croatia is painfully clear – Croats are a genocidal nation. And "amin" [amen in Serbian]. Unfortunately, Croatia cannot be informed about that at all, let alone define a permanent politics towards Serbia that would respond to such provocations. Mutual meetings at the highest levels were used in the post-Tuđman period for nonsense and "apologies". Moreover, the Croatian regime's own moves frequently feed the Greater Serbian politics towards Croatia.

There is an entire workflow which proves that it is a case of systematic politics. The regime agreed to push the 1996 Agreement on Normalization of Relations under the rug. Then it guaranteed three Parliamentary representatives from the SDSS party – the party founded by a Greater Serbian war criminal. Then, such SDSS became a factor in coalition governments – the authority. The amnesty of crimes began with simultaneous condemnation of Croatian veterans. And then it went in the direction of Croatia paying war compensation to the participants in the aggression on Croatia (which was called a program for the return of refugees, so that Croats did not figure out the truth). Active aggressors became government factors. Anti-Croatian propaganda is heavily financed from the state budget.… The Greater Serbian politics in Croatia has no chance if it does not have the fifth columnists in Croatia. But it does, it does.

And then, within such internal circumstances directed by the regime, there came the Serbian exhibition in the UN, which advertised at a global level not the Greater Serbian, but precisely the Serbian myth of Jasenovac, including the negation of Stepinac. A direct culprit for that misdeed is also the Croatian regime. The regime that on the internal plan finances films of which the Greater Serbian propaganda machine would not be ashamed, theatre performances of which even Hitler's anti-Semitic machinery would not be ashamed. Why did the regime not stimulate an objective, scientific research of Jasenovac? Is it so that Serbia even in the twenty-first century can spin out the Jasenovac myth and thesis about the genocidal Croatian nation?

And so, we arrive to the "verbal war", which was spotted from the Pantovčak [presidential office] hunter check station by the advisory body to the President of the Republic of Croatia. The war that the President wants to abolish with the invitation to Vučić on the eve of Stepinac feast day. However, there is no war. Not even a verbal war. There is, however, the pushing under the rug of the implementation of the 1996 Agreement on Normalization. The Croatian regime carries equal guilt for its un-implementation during twenty-two years. In some phases, it openly favored the Belgrade politics towards Croatia, even to the point that it financed and staffed it.

And in such a way that a Serbian intelligence agent, at the time of the Greater Serbia aggression on Croatia, was placed in a position from which he made decisions about the cultural politics of the Republic of Croatia, while a Croatian intelligence agent with Serbian nationality was publicly denounced. While such circumstances prevail, Vučić has practically nothing to do in Zagreb, except supervise if everything is going according to Plan (Serb. *Načertanije* = Cro. Plan). Altogether unnecessarily, with the political maneuver of the President of the Government – and not on the electoral basis, we arrived at a point today where the Croatian government depends on the notorious Pupovac. That is, the modern Svetozar Pribićević, before his last, Parisian political phase.

Let's return to Stepinac. When the negators of Stepinac's role in World War II no longer know what to say under the burden of historical documents, there are only two platitudes left to them. Well, he did not do enough. Well, he was not saving people under threat to his life. Only to then knock it all together into a single argument – Stepinac was not proclaimed Righteous Among the Nations. That thesis is used also by Belgrade manipulators. Let's have a look at Ljubica Štefan's research to see what it's all about (*Stepinac and the Jews,* Croatiaproject, Zagreb 1998).

The proposal that Yad Vashem proclaim Alojzije Stepinac Righteous Among the Nations was submitted on 10 March 1994 by two Jews, Dr Amiel Shomrony and Dr Igor Primorac. It is necessary to fulfill two conditions in order to become Righteous Among the Nations. The first is to have saved at least one Jew from certain death, about which there was no doubt in Stepinac's case. The second is that in saving that life, their own was in put peril. In Stepinac's case that was and still is doubtful today, thanks to Miriam Steiner-Aviezer, a Jew of Yugoslav orientation.

Dr Schomrony and Dr Primorac's proposal was supported in 1995 by the Croatian Academy of Science and Arts, the Croatian Archive, the Institute of Contemporary History, the Croatian Victimological Association and a group of Croatian Righteous Among the Nations, among whom was also the Righteous Ljubica Štefan.

Steiner-Aviezer was a member of the Commission that decided about Stepinac. She was the only one who understood Croatian, the language in which most of the documents were written. Her view was as follows: "Stepinac might have saved individuals, but to save an entire old people's home he needed the approval of the Ustasha authorities, publicly or tacitly, and that speaks against him". OK. If that is the criterion. Dr

Mordecai Paldiel, director of the Yad Vashem Office for the Righteous Among Nations, declared that the following is written in the documents: "We are a Jewish country, therefore, we cannot give a medal to a Cardinal of the Catholic Church". He added that the fact that Stepinac survived the war indicates that his life was not in danger while protecting and saving Jews. OK again, if that it so, let it be so.

That rule, surviving the war, was introduced, it seems, only for Cardinal Stepinac. In agreement with the police, the Greek Orthodox Church Patriarch Papandreou Damaskinos converted Greek Jews to Christianity, instructed priests to help them and approved pro-forma Christian-Jewish marriages. He was not proclaimed a Nazi collaborator because of that. Patriarch Damaskinos survived the war. During the war he did not experience public attack in the press, threatening letters, stoning, or assassination attempts. The Jews publicly express their gratitude and recognition to him.

Oskar Schindler also survived the war. During the war, he had a factory within an SS camp complex. He cooperated with the SS and the Gestapo. He did not persecute the Jews, but took care of them because he benefited with their work in the factory. He died a Righteous man Among the Nations, but it is not known when and where his life was in danger.

As a Catholic, I am entirely indifferent about the criteria on which the medal of Righteousness is awarded. However, as a Croat, I am not indifferent when uneven criteria are used to measure a Croat rescuer of Jews in relation to rescuers of other nationalities. So, the above argument against Stepinac not being proclaimed Righteous as proof that he could have done more than he did, and that his life was not threatened, has to be seen with sober eyes. And not be misled by storytelling, although here everybody "is telling stories" but says ever less.

Stepinac was investigated twice (in 1970 and 1996) and he was denied twice. He was credited with some merit for rescuing Jews from an old people's home and for saving converted Jews. However, Iris Rosenberg, the spokeswoman of the Yad Vashem Museum, on 14 May 1998 wrote - "persons who helped Jews, but who cooperated or were closely related to fascist regimes that participated in Nazi persecutions of Jews, can be denied the title of Righteous".

Giorgio Perlesca, however, was not denied the title! The following criterion was valid for him: "Had Giorgio Perlesca not been a fascist, he would not have had the opportunity to save 3-6,000 Hungarian Jews". That was written by Eric Silver, Jewish publicist in his book published in 1992, based on the data collected from the archives of the Yad Vashem Museum. In that book he analyzes fourty persons proclaimed as Righteous. He also mentions Oskar Schindler, member of the National-Socialist Party and Hitler's counter-intelligence person. Patriarch Damaskinos cooperated with the Greek police boss, that is, with the regime that had to be loyal to the German occupier. Georg Duckwitz was a Naval attaché in the German embassy in Denmark, member of the National-Socialist Party. Max Schmeling served in the parachute troops of Wehrmacht. And so on.

The "Ustasha vicar" label that was stuck on Stepinac was the work of the joint Greater Serbian and Yugo-communist continued efforts in "these areas", but what is more important in the world too. They have confused even the current Pope! They work non-stop on that task in order to calumniate the Croats internationally. And they spend as much money on that as necessary. Even today Serbia feverishly hangs on to those historically rotten lianas, but rotten or not, they produce results. The first is, by continuous strikes on Croatia, to draw attention as far as possible from questioning their own unclean historical conscience and their role in the extermination of Jews. The second is to prevent Croatia's normal development on the basis of her identity, and to force it into an eternally defensive position while waiting for a convenient moment for territorial expansion.

Should President Kolinda Grabar-Kitarović take advantage of her meeting with Vučić and switch to counter attack, to the field of historical facts without any Yugoslav backlogs and complexes, to the field of the concluded Agreement on Normalisation, whose implementation is the only possible way to reach normalisation in the relations between the two States, then this meeting with the declared Chetnik with an unclean conscience could perhaps make sense. That is also clear to Vučić, so before coming to Croatia, and in order to avoid the trap of de-mythologized ground, he wished for a six-month "moratorium on historical topics". He too, in fact, understood the little stories and mantras, but also the opportunity of the "European path" and "European perspectives" so that we forget the past and switch to the future, Europe does not have an alternative, let us be inclusive, let us build mainstream politics on the path of Western Balkans strategy, that is, "who the hell made us quarrel" with conglomerates of bad politics and so on. Round and round.

In projections of Greater Serbia, and Serbia is working only on that and nothing else, Vučić blew the Republic of Serbian Krajina. He also blew Kosovo. He only has the Serbian Republic, established on genocide, left. Thanks to the disastrous politics of the Third January regime, he still has a fairly realistic hope that in Croatia he can renew the pre-requisites to establish relations such as they were until the democratic changes in 1990. They have already been partially established. For example, the current Minister of Foreign Affairs previously worked for the Serbian government, although it is somehow a custom that Ministers work for foreign governments as advisors only after the end of their career. The reverse order directly contradicts the criteria of national security. Luckily, the President did not have to pass any previous exam in Belgrade before she became President.

Vučić hopes that he will achieve the phantasmagorical Greater Serbia with the help of the European Union, just as Ranković hoped that he would achieve it with the help of Yalta and Staljin, or as Nedić hoped that he would establish it with the help of Hitler and Mussolini, and just as the monarch hoped that he would establish it with the help of Versailles and the dictatorship. With his arrival to Zagreb on the wings of the globally extended Jasenovac and anti-Stepinac myth, Vučić will try to play the role of Tito, little Tito, the boss of the Western Balkans, or, as the Croatian communists would put it – "our most loved guest". If that happens, the President has only one choice – a kick in the back side.

In other words, if Vučić comes with a modified platform of unity or death, he should be received with the platform of the Agreement on Normalization or march home. Since he was invited to "embellish" our Stepinac feast day.

(hkv.hr, 7 February 2018.)

     A century of Serbian terror 1918 - 2018

The Serbs are "endangered" for as long as they do not become a political entity and fulfill their right to secession

President Kolinda Grabar-Kitarović and Serbian President Aleksandar Vučić visited yesterday the students of the Politacademy of the Serbian National Council and the presentation of the project *The future of Serbs in Croatia* in the Zagreb-Ljubljana Metropolitanate of the Serbian Orthodox Church in Croatia. In company of the Orthodox high school students, they met Metropolitan Porfirije. He told them: "I am delighted with your disposition and the words of responsibility with which you addressed the nations. Serbs and Croats have always been directed towards each other. Unfortunately, the times were such that we became distanced and that is why this step forward is an invitation for peace and understanding. President Vučić, your visit is an encouragement to our people who live here and who are afraid and live in a kind of apathy, giving up on themselves".

One of the most concrete results of Vučić's arrival in Zagreb is the updating, at the highest level, of the cult of the endangered Serbs in Croatia, whom Porfirije, in the middle of Zagreb, calls a "nation", thus the holders of statehood with the right to secession. He does it right into the face of the protectress of the Constitution of the Republic of Croatia. The protectress – blinked at that, as could be seen on TV. However, it could not be heard what was the future of Serbs in Croatia. If they are endangered, then they have to be helped to get out of peril. How? By paying war compensation. They are not satisfied with the amounts so far.

Porfirije converted, without hesitation, a national minority into a nation. And he presented that nation as living in fear. The Serbs in Croatia are not a nation. The Serbs also do not have any reason to live in fear, unless Porfirije brain-washes them into believing it. His speech is in full harmony with the "endangering" about which our political elites do not know enough. For that reason, the people immediately called them beginners. The endangered status is one of the most important components of the Greater Serbian ideology. It is possible to speak about the cult of the endangered Serb in Croatia from different points of view: historical, journalist, satirical, political....

The endangering of Serbianism and the Serbs, however, is a "dominant idea of Serbian politics since the 1878 Berlin Congress. Since then politics have been controlled from Belgrade and included all neighboring states... Political parties were created in Croatia, financed by the Serbian government (the most significant is the Serbian Independent Party). One of the key elements of the ideology of those parties is the 'endangering' of Serbs" – Dr Mato Artuković wrote in his work *Endangering* – the important element in Greater Serbian ideology. The pumping of the endangered status has a specific goal: mobilization of an endangered people in Croatia to whom the Croat does not allow statehood with the right of secession. Integral Croatia, as a state, does not exist in the Greater Serbian ideology, which is in many aspects embedded in the official Belgrade politics.

The root of the conflict between Croats and Serbs in the nineteenth century comes down to a different view of the idea of a state. Serbs in Croatia consider that in addition to Serbia, "Serbian states" include also Montenegro, Kosovo, Macedonia, and Bosnia and Herzegovina. Besides these states according to that construction, Dalmatia, Lika, Krbava, Banovina, Slavonia and Srijem are also Serbian on the grounds of historical and natural rights. And that is the start of the story which they are spinning still today, even in Christmas greetings in which they avoid to say Croatia. That should be the introduction ("a small step") into the first grade for Croatian beginners. The Chetniks, though, know all about that – it is all they do, so this must be boring for them to read.

Anyway, to be absolutely clear, how can Serbia be the aggressor on Dalmatia, Lika, Krbava, Banovina, Slavonia and Srijem, if they are Serbian states? Operation Storm is the aggression! That is why Vučić says that we do not agree on anything related to the "past". Not on history, but the past, which unlike history, can be this way or that, depending on who is the first to investigate it, and if the investigation comes from the Serbian side, then the new rule is valid - *ćeraćemo se još* [we will chase each other again]. Those "investigations" and "chasings" are even today a part of the official politics of the Serbian state towards Croatia. Vučić demonstrated that very well yesterday, while lining up Croatian democratic legitimacies and Cardinal Bozanić, misused for a great Western Balkans party, by which in a Yugoslav way, Zagreb is opening the door for Belgrade to join

A century of Serbian terror 1918 - 2018

the EU. That siren is a two-way call. The President has at the same time shut the door on her second term. For whom is she preparing the job in Pantovčak? For Milanović, Josipović...?

The story, our dear first-graders, could be shortened in the following set of ideas, which you must learn by heart straightaway, like the times table or the alphabet: if we, the Serbs, are not a political nation in Dalmatia, Lika, Krbava, Banovina, Slavonia and Srijem, then we are unequal. If we are unequal, then we are endangered. Who is endangering us in these regions? The Croats. Who are the Croats? If they do not want to be Serbs of Catholic "religion", which we have generously offered, if they do not want to be the paid Belgrade slaves, except for a few honourable exceptions, then they are a genocidal nation, because they are permanently endangering us in the western Serbian regions. If they are a genocidal nation, and they are, they must be because our folk songs and "history", the Serbian Church and the UN exhibition say so, then they must apologize permanently, continuously ask for "forgiveness" and forever be paying us for their eastern "sin of sins". The sin consists only of the fact that the Croats have survived on their own. To be a political people [nation] on somebody else's territory is the goal of the Serbian endangering cult.

In 1848, Jovan Živković, a paid agent of the Serbian government, organised Serbian politics in Croatia. Between him and Milorad Pupovac many years have passed, during which one can follow the development of the cult of Serbian endangering and its continual renewal in different political circumstances. That is apparent ranging from the Srbobran newspaper (which was paid by the Serbian government) to the current *Novosti* newspaper, which is paid by the Croatian government. Accompanied by anti-Croatian "satire". The Serbian press in Croatia, permanently present for almost 150 years, brings out ideological articles of the Greater Serbian ideology and the Serbian cult of Saint Sava. The Croats are presented as inhuman people in those articles. However, "One of the permanent elements in the ideological structure of all those so-called opposition Serbian journals and the whole publishing activity is also anti-Semitism" (M. Artuković, *idem*).

The Serbian press in Croatia has long been accusing and blaming everything that is Croatian, aiming to proclaim the entire nation guilty.

The targets are the nobility, the church, the clergy, the Parliament, Croatian institutions… up to today's tabloid titles "both, both, they both fell"[38], the ritual slaughter of M.P. Thompson, the ridicule of the Croatian anthem, and so on. Dubrovnik and its writers are not "Serbian" since yesterday, they are Serbian since the middle of the nineteenth century. Sima Lukin Lazić was one of the key "editors" in Croatia. "He Serbianised three quarters of the face of the earth. Although he was a bitter anti-Semite… he proclaimed Jesus a Serb" (M. Artuković, *idem*). Insanity? No, the system. Totalitarian. More long-lived and more lasting than communism.

The cult of the endangered Serbs is eternal. It lives simultaneously in the past, the present and in the future. It is irrational, continuous, constantly perpetuated. The extent of a Serb's endangerment in Croatia is illustrated by the fact that at the beginning of the twentieth century the *Srbobran* newspaper published the article by Nikola Stojanović *Serbs and Croats* inspired by the predecessors of national-socialism and racism in the Hitler mould. It is a programmatic article on Serbianism in Croatia for the entire twentieth century. With the message "until the investigation, ours or yours"!

At the end of the twentieth century, after a series of Serbian defeats in Croatia, Matija Bećković published the poem *Ćeraćemo se još* [We will be chasing each other again], intended for the twenty-first century. Why? Because yesterday and today they wanted to be a political people in Dalmatia, Lika, Krbava, Banovina, Slavonia and Srijem. In Croatia. Once they become *politički narod* [a nation, political entity], they will head for secessions and "annexations", as we have seen in recent history, sorry – the "past", on which we do not agree, but by taking "small steps" we will, sooner or later, perhaps even before that.

In the twentieth century, the cult of endangered Serbs reached "cosmic" dimensions with the myth about Jasenovac and the 700,000 (up to two million) killed Serbs. The Serbian myth on Jasenovac converted the crime of the Ustasha regime and the as yet undetermined number of

---

38 *Both, both, they both fell* is the spontaneous exclamation of delight in a video of one of the legendary events of the Homeland War in September 1991, when two enemy JNA aircraft were shot down; its short version 'Both fell' still has an association with success in the collective memory.

A century of Serbian terror 1918 - 2018

deaths among camp prisoners of different nationalities, which cannot be larger than a few thousand but could be less than that number, into a crime that would only have been possible if the entire Croatian population had participated in it. That is why Serbia insists on 700,000. They could not care less about the victims; they want a global label of the genocidal character of the Croatian people. A responsible government not subject to the complexes of the Greater Serbian and Yugo-communist ideology would solve that problem in the only possible scientifically objective way. But, what would Pupovac be doing in Croatia then? Why the *Novosti* newspaper then? All would end up "in pieces". If Croats are not a genocidal nation, then the Serbs in Croatia cannot become a political nation with the right to secession.

The cult of Serb endangerment in Croatia is the basis of the Serbian exhibition at the UN. It is the basis of Vučić's howling about the lack of sewage infrastructure in some "parts" of their never materialized dream of Western Serbian regions, the basis of Pupovac's pretence howling, the basis of the editing policy of the *Novosti* newspaper, the basis of journalistic and theatre "satire" of contemporary sorcerers and the basis of Porfirije's statement on "our people" in Croatia – "frightened and they live in a kind of apathy". They cannot be frightened. Well, Pupovac is the authority in Croatia. However, if they suffer collective apathy (which nobody with any common sense believes), then it is so because despite the aggression committed, they did not become a political nation in Dalmatia, Lika, Krbava, Banovina, Slavonia and Srijem. On top of which, their "homeland" is due to pay war compensation, and deal with the definition of borders, the issue of the missing persons in Serbian concentration camps, the issue of national minorities, and the issue of the return of the stolen treasure....

The nourishing of the cult of Serbian endangerment has a long history in Croatia. Unfortunately, that cult is apparently only taught in the Serbian-Orthodox institutions and at the Political Academy of Pupovac's Serbian National Council. OK, if necessary, also by certain professors at the School of Philosophy and at the Political "Sciences". In the places where the duration of the cult of endangering Serbs is being extended. A rational person cannot see it. After all, the "endangering" was the basis of the aggression on Croatia by Serbia and Montenegro, including allied rebelled Serbs. This is not mentioned in textbooks. At whose expense? For whose benefit?

The President of the Republic of Croatia is perhaps not aware, although she should be, about the origin of the deceitful, apparently harmless endangering. Neither that the ruinous creation of the Jasenovac myth was produced from the cult of endangering. Here is an illustrative example of how that is done. In 1991 "at Easter time", an epistle of the Serbian Orthodox Church was published. When you finish reading it, dear readers, try to forget about the past and turn to a future of imposing endangering with the help of "small steps", such as the one, for example, that Mr Metropolitan took.

Quote: "To what extent has the killing of our people during the last fifty years been so much more numerous and more terrible? During four years, not less than 700,000 persons, if not more, were killed in Jasenovac only. If we ask in which way this happened, one of our excellent scientists and thinkers responds: 'Jasenovac is the greatest place of horror for Serbs, the place of annihilation, of extermination, of execution, where people were crushed by bloodthirstiness, such that certainly not even the Duke of Demons can remember. It is the new crucifixion of Christ. It is the sin of sins. That is the reason why this unparalleled crime has remained remorseless and unrepented to this day, which is confirmed by the events that happen even today in the same place and by the same perpetrators".

"In the same place and by the same perpetrators"! That was in 1991. Today's Croatia is removing the monument to Croatian veterans who opposed this monstrous "epistle", the cult of endangering and its consequences, from Jasenovac. Because it allegedly offends the feelings of the "victim nation" (M. Pupovac).

Metropolite Porfirije is certainly familiar with the thoughts of Nikolaj, bishop of Žiča. They are embedded in the so-called "Easter" epistle of the Serbian Orthodox Church: "Should the Serbs retaliate in the same measure for all the crimes that they endured in this century, what should they do?" This is what the allegedly endangered Serbs should do, and we remember that they did exactly that, namely, the most bestial crimes: "They should bury people alive, they should roast people alive on spits, they should peel the skin off form living people, and they should cut children into pieces in front of their parents. The Serbs have never done that. Not even to animals, let alone to people".

Perhaps they did not do that to "animals". They did it to Croats, but then, according to the "criterion" of the endangered Serb cult, Croats (and let's not forget the Jews) are not people. However, that is how criminal and totalitarian ideologies are built.

Notorious substitutions of theses and forgeries are embedded in the cult of endangering – attribute the crimes you committed to the victim and carry on. All is justified in the name of endangering. The ideology of endangering exempts the criminal of responsibility in advance. That vicious circle can be broken only if Serbia is forced to pay war compensation. Tuđman prepared a good base in that regard. But for whom? His successors are taking "small steps" to Croatia's detriment (the live frog cooking technique)[39]. They are also making increasingly more concessions for the renewal of the Greater Serbian ideology and the institutionalization of the "political people". That is why Porfirije could not refrain but cheerfully exclaim: "I am delighted with your disposition and the words of responsibility with which you addressed the nations". Na-ti-on-s. No chance that he could pronounce "Serbian national minority in Croatia". His "religion" does not allow it. Onward to Greater Serbia.

Behind lowered blinds, the Croats have been thoroughly shamed yesterday and today. Within two days, the regime has forbidden them to hold two protests, yesterday in Zagreb and today in Gvozd. In which of the European Union nations does that happen? Luckily, no Grgo Anđelinović fired at them. In their misfortune, they wanted to protest against Vučić's story in Glina in 1995. At the time, he was convincing the rebel Serbs that by occupying Glina they had forever stopped being endangered. Today, alas, he must convince them that they are endangered again. I have no idea if that was the reason for his invite from the President. The installation of Serbian endangering is the first visible result of Vučić's visit to Croatia.

---

39 In 2004 Krešimir Sever, President of the Independent Croatian Trade Unions, drew a parallel between the absence of protests to the escalating cost of living in Croatia and the method of cooking a live frog by starting with cold water so that it gets used to the rising temperature and eventually cooks without jumping out.

Everything, except Vučić's encounter with Plenković, should be forgotten as soon as possible and rejected with disdain. In order that we do not fall into "apathy and giving up ourselves".

(hkv.hr, 13 February 2018.)

Renewal of Yugoslavia according to Euro-Chetnik criteria

The Yugoslav totalitarian communist Day of the Republic was celebrated on 29 November 2017 in The Hague with the verdict to six Croatians. From its creation until its collapse and afterwards, the Republic of Yugoslavia is considered by the Serbs as territory of the Greater Serbia, with its northern border on the river Sutla. The verdict proclaimed Croatia as aggressor on Bosnia and Herzegovina for defending it from the project of a Greater Serbia. Because of such injustice, General Praljak committed suicide in front of the entire world before the pronunciation of the complete verdict and marked forever the international introduction to the centenary celebration of Yugoslavia.

Three months later, on 12 February 2018 the Yugoslav partying continued in Zagreb with the visit of Serbian President Aleksandar Vučić, notorious Chetnik and active aggressor on Croatia. The visit was used to forget the "past" and to turn to the future. It is clear that Greater Serbia is still today's vision for Vučić and the Serbian state, which every ordinary and averagely informed citizen knew even without the two-day partying. A great assembly was held in the Lisinski Concert Hall, which looked like a "people's event" of the rebel Serbs on the eve of the aggression on Croatia. The victim nation of the criminal operation Storm and of the vampire-like Ustasha was being honed. Once it is honed, the daggers are sharpened and cockades pulled out from under the mattress and polished. There was talk about reconciliation of the people, but here the Serbian national minority has to reconcile with the idea that they are a national minority in Croatia.

The highest government institutions received Vučić: President of the Republic of Croatia, President of the Government of the Republic of Croatia, President of the Croatian Parliament. Even Cardinal Josip Bozanić.

The apologists on duty tried to find ingenious reasons to objectively justify the unjustifiable visit. They mentioned new geostrategic rearrangements as the reason for Vučić's visit. If there are such rearrangements, Croatia should participate in them as a subject, rather than as a Chetnik object. Undoubtedly, Croatia suffered a shock on both 29 November last year and on 12 February this year. For a definition of shock, consult a dictionary. The apologists to the current duty restorers want to say that shocks are for the Croatian common good. The excellent Serbian poet Branko Miljković (Niš, 1934 – Zagreb, 1961) would say: "Fallacies are their best songs".

The marking of the centenary of the Yugoslav unification (1 December 1918 – 1 December 2018) will continue until the end of the year. I have nothing against nostalgia and Yugo-sentimentality, as long as the celebrations do not become a reconstruction. And they have become a reconstruction of Yugoslavia in all shapes and forms long ago. This is not even hidden anymore. But it is forbidden to speak about the reconstruction in decision-making places and in public. The decision-making places and the leading media in Croatia have been thoroughly cleaned-up of historical memory, common sense and of persons who stick to the principle – Our all for Croatia, Croatia at any cost[40].

The renewed Yugoslavia, Euroslavia, as it now looks, will rest on the same principles as the monarchist and Yugo-communist Yugoslavia. It will balance between the East and West. Serbia will be the leader and bearer of the "school cane", Croatia will be a submissive and obedient maid – Alija Sirotanović's[41] coal fuelled locomotive until Serbia's entry into the European Union. Until the entry, Croatia must position the Serbian

---

40 The famous words of Croatia's first president Dr Franjo Tuđman: *Uvijek i sve za Hrvatsku, a našu jedinu i vječnu Hrvatsku ni za što!* Always and all for our Croatia, and our only and eternal Croatia at any cost! They were abbreviated into a patriotic much used phrase *Sve za Hrvatsku, Hrvatsku nizašto!* Our all for Croatia, Croatia at any cost!

41 Alija Sirotanović (1914-1990) was a coal miner in Breza, SFRJ, who defeated the world record in 1949 by digging up 154 tonnes of coal in 8 hours with his fellow miners. He was presented to Marshall Tito, asking apparently only for a larger shovel. Their effort was honured with his image printed on the 20,000 dinars note in 1987.

issue on the highest level and resolve it from that level in accordance with peace and stability in the Western Balkans. That is why Plenković holds Pupovac in his arms, and Grabar-Kitarović does so with Vučić. There are no other open issues regarding the renewal. If there are any, then they belong to the *laprdientia croatica* [Croatian piffle] section.

It is essential for a quality renewal to continuously depreciate the foundations of the Croatian state, the Homeland War and regularly strike to shock the Croatian people to such an extent that they "give up on themselves" (Porfirije), because only then Serbia and the Serbs in Croatia can cure their feelings of military and diplomatic defeat by that true Croatian Croatia. In that regard, the paradigmatic statements with long-lasting consequences are also valid. Such as Sanader's statement – "Hristos is born" or Kolinda Grabar-Kitarović's – "This is your Homeland". Once expressed, the "political people" in the Serbian national minority turn them into an unquestionable standard and a measure for evaluating everybody and everything.

The renewal process in Croatia lasts from 3 January 2000. It's a matter of continuity in giving up the military victories, the diplomatic successes, freedom, all the way up to state subjectivity and national dignity. Its' execution is helped by the betrayal by Croatian Judas and the high treason of Yugoslav Yudas in the "stone by stone" Garašanin tactic, and from 12 February 2018 the "politics of small steps". All factors that created the previous two Yugoslavias are included in the renewal, including the Croatian fifth column, the Chetniks and the so called "international community". Since the processes of renewal have been taking place, the position of Croats in Bosnia and Herzegovina has been getting worse. The official Serbian view yesterday, today and tomorrow sees and encourages the extinction and emptying out of entire territories in Croatia of remaining sovereign bearers, that is, the "Ustasha". In the next version of Yugoslavia, Euroslavia, Croats are destined to extinction to the point from where there is no recovery. Then the Western Balkans will be peaceful and stable "forever".

The key internal document on which the reconstruction of a better past is based, is Račan's proposal of June 1991 that Croatia must simultaneously proclaim both its independence and its entering into negotiations on the renewal of Yugoslavia, which, thanks to God, was rejected at the time. Due to that proposal, he became the head of government nine years later. As head of government, he immediately set up the foundations of the renewal. After he did not fall due to the Western Balkans Summit in Zagreb in November 2000, it was clear that a series of new shocks were to follow along the lines of weakening the state, manufacture of fog and production of a renewal agreement. His policy of renewal is being conducted to this day through several different tactical versions. The execution of the biggest shocks is left to the mandates when the Yugo-communists are not formally in power. When they are formally in power, they mark the path to renewal. They leave the dirtiest jobs on the renewal to "political opponents". Oh, my Fancek [Franjo Tuđman]!

The next fatal date, after The Hague 29 November 2017 and Zagreb 12 February 2018, has not as yet been announced to Croats in order that the shock produces the greatest effect within the depth and breadth of the Croatian nation. These two well-known dates have thoroughly humiliated the Homeland War, the Croatian state and Croatian people in Bosnia and Herzegovina and in Croatia. A new date is hurriedly being prepared, as Aleksandar Vučić and Kolinda Grabar-Kitarović have informed us. The renewal, in other words, must not be stopped. The state of shock must be exploited to the maximum.

The strategy for the Western Balkans has been approved, planned, staffed and politically equipped at an international level, just as Tito's "revolution" once was. In Serbia, leaders with a Chetnik background are accepted. In Croatia, leaders of the Croatian silence are being installed, with pronounced Yugoslav complexes, the minimalists. In the synergy of Chetniks and minimalists, the renewal has a good chance to succeed. Just as in 1985, for example, it was difficult for an average Croat to believe that only a couple of years later Croatia would become a free country, so it is difficult today to believe, in spite of advanced renewal, that in a couple of years Croatia could also formally disappear as an international subject. With Pupovac it does not have an ordered internal politics, or with Blažeković a foreign politics. People can basically trust only in God's help. Nobody mentions elections anymore.

It is important that "peace and stability" are not disrupted during the renewal. Only the Chetnik element can maintain Serbia peaceful and stable. That is why the last two Serbian presidents are explicit Chetniks, participants in the aggression on Croatia, and even the third one, who was not formally a Chetnik, behaved like a Chetnik towards Croatia. Only a more or less treacherous element can maintain Croatia peaceful and stable regarding the renewal.

Serbia's starting positions are well known in this game. Unchangeable since the time of Ilija Garašanin. In real time that means: we were not the aggressors; we were defending Yugoslavia together with the international community. In the Western Balkans, in the regions where they are not a political nation, the Serbs are endangered. The endangering of Serbs is a threat to peace and stability. It is necessary to establish such relations in the Western Balkans that Serbia can control peace and stability. That could be settled the way it was settled in Yugoslavia – all Serbs in one state. The problem are the genocidal Croats. They do not want Yugoslav relations. They are "ever since and forever" the perturbing factor for peace and stability. The disposition of the majority in Croatia must be declared as marginal and extreme. It would be best for the renewal that this is done by Croatian elites under Belgrade supervision. The renewal will be carried out more easily if Serbs in Croatia become a *politički narod* [nation, political entity] with their own territory and with the right to secession.

The Croatian starting positions for renewal are also clear: we cannot do it overnight. We can do it with small steps. We have to at the same time invest a lot of energy on the internal plan in the stability of renewal forces, especially on the deception that renewal is not possible. Sorry, but we have to mention once a year that aggression was committed on Croatia. We apologize for the fact that we have the Ministry of Croatian Veterans. We agree that Milošević's regime is guilty for the aggression, not Serbia. It is not yet the right time to also blame Tuđman's regime for your aggression on us. We are in the European Union, but brothers, that only means that the entry of Serbia into the European Union is a Croatian stretegic goal and nothing else. Do not worry, everything will be all right. We must not renew more rapidly due to internal circumstances, so from time to time, please understand, we have to repeat – "the wounds are still fresh".

For Serbia, the renewal according to Euro-Chetnik "criteria" is convenient. Not for the Croats. Nobody is to be held responsible

A century of Serbian terror 1918 - 2018

for the renewal before the Croatian people and voters. The evasion of responsibility is carried out first by establishing a system in which nobody is responsible for anything, which still Račan achieved without any resistance by changing everything that did or could eventually disturb the renewal. When the executive power exaggerates with the pace of the renewal, the relay baton must be taken by the judicial, legislative or presidential power. And so round and round.

The burden of renewal must not be predominantly on one side of the government, but has to be distributed evenly to create an illusion that the renewal is a regular condition of the state and the nation. In order to maintain such a system, it is necessary to have a suitable electoral legislation and preserve it "like the apple of one's eye". The renewal must be carried out in accordance with the law. The law must be in service of the renewal. And the whole legislation must be aligned with the European Union Western Balkans strategy. Especially the staff, because staff politics, as Lenin put it, is the mother of all politics.

Where is Croatia in this? It is nowhere. Where are Croatian people in this? They are nowhere.

(hkv.hr, 20 February 2018)

The crisis of truth in Croatian-Serbian relations

In 1990, Tuđman's all-Croatian reconciliation was promoted in Croatia. The Serbs in Croatia rejected it in a plebiscite. The remnants of the Yugoslav totalitarian regime accepted it with fingers crossed in their pockets hoping it will not work out. As followers of Belgrade's Greater Serbia platform, which in Croatia ended with defeat and the collective rout, the Serbs were the greatest losers in refusing the reconciliation. The remnants of the Yugo-communist totalitarian regime were smarter. They waited and in the background of war events prepared for the counter-attack moment. The Croatian people established a national state with a long delay and it seemed that it sobered up from costly Yugoslav fallacies.

However, in 2000 – Tuđman's concept of reconciliation was replaced by Račan's revanchism. It simultaneously settled accounts with the bearers of Croatian state independence and opened doors to the Serbs in Croatia in the sense of resetting starting positions with which they went into war against Croatia. The Serbs accepted Račan's revanchism. In the atmosphere of revanchism, the anti-dialogue of the "ghost of the past" emerged, the renewed single-mindedness – which today we call mainstream, and we justify with political stability and inclusiveness. The principle of truth is replaced by the renewal of single-mindedness.

All this led to a crisis of truth in the Croatian-Serbian relations, which Kolinda Grabar-Kitarović and Aleksandar Vučić admitted to in Zagreb in 2018, when they determined that they did not agree on anything relating to the past and on that basis "opened a new page in mutual relations". And they decided to normalize relations between the two states with the tactics of "small steps", leaving aside the 1996 Agreement on Normalization. Without resolving the crisis of truth, however, any tactic is condemned to failure and the repetition of historical fallacies. In place of yesterday's Serbian occupation, we obtained its reintegration into the government. I am incapable of estimating which is worse.

On which side is the Serbian national minority regarding the truth on recent history? If we consider the political behavior of Milorad Pupovac, his followers and the media, then it is obvious that their political position is on the Belgrade side, and their wallet deep inside the Croatian budget. The problem is that much greater for the fact that the Serbian national minority, although disagreeing with the fundamental truths that underlie the Croatian state, is deeply embedded in the Croatian government. This pushes up the further course in the crisis of truth, without which there is no justice and real reconciliation, but at the same time, a space is opened for continuous revanchism towards the bearers of the Croatian state renewal.

Can those parties who diametrically oppose the causes of the war, the character of the war and the military-police operations Bljesak [Flash] and Oluja [Storm] participate in the Croatian Government? That is, if operation Storm is a crime, then the Serbian aggression on Croatia is a liberating action. If Croatia is fascist, then the Republic of Serbian Krajina – RSK is democratic. There should be no compromise on these divisions. Consequently, can the relations between the two states be consolidated if Serbia does not accept the basic truth that it committed aggression on Croatia? They cannot.

A century of Serbian terror 1918 - 2018

Since there has, nevertheless, been a compromise and a reconciliation of irreconcilable views, it is logical that Pupovac requires even more from the compromise achieved. He wants the status of a constituent nation, a political nation. He also wants Serbian territory in Croatia. And with this he actually identifies himself as a restorer of ideas that are contained in the very essence of the Greater Serbian aggression on Croatia. That would not be tragic, since the Croatian Croatia knows how to solve that problem, had he not been seconded by the Croatian Government. It does nothing to suppress the renewal of myths on which the aggression was initiated. On the contrary. It does everything to make the restorers "feel good". And the proof that they feel good is Pupovac in the Government, the *Novosti* newspaper on a grant instead of the market, and the great assembly in the Lisinski Hall.

As far as the Croatian Croatia is concerned, the basis of Greater Serbia can no longer be a guarantor of "stability and peace", a guarantor of overcoming the crisis of truth and establishing justice. Reconciliation is possible only with truth. On the other hand, neither can the Yugoslav fogs, to which the Croatian political elite resorts, contribute to overcome the crisis of truth in the Croatian-Serbian relations. What seems to be essential is that the Serbs in Croatia accept the position of a national minority like all other national minorities - only in that way can they become a subject of respect, while the Croatian state should admit that it must behave just like any other sovereign state – as a subject. That is the minimum, the prerequisite, the small step needed to overcome the crisis of truth in the Croatian-Serbian relations. Truth is the basis on which the Croatian – Serb relations in Croatia and those between Croatia and Serbia can be normalized. On nothing else.

The Croatian parties and the parties in Croatia are wrong in thinking that they will overcome the crisis of truth with the help of the so-called international community or the European Union. All Serbian myths from Garašanin to this day have survived in the crucial moments precisely with the help of the international community.

It has to be clearly explained to the so-called international community, that in the interpretation of Serbian politicians and media, the Croats were a genocidal nation long before the Greater Serbianism in the Yugo-communist wing created the myth of Jasenovac. I doubt that the

Government, the Parliament and Pantovčak [the Presidency] worry about that. Their standards in current policy, unless they are directed by remote control from the outside, have the character of a frog's perspective.

Since when, then, is the Croatian nation continually genocidal towards the Serbs? "For centuries"! Serbian academic Vasilije Krestić in his article *On the Genesis of the Genocide on Serbs in the Independent State of Croatia – NDH,* published in *Književne Novine* newspaper dated 15 September 1986, claims that: "It is totally certain that the genesis of the genocidal actions on Serbs in Croatia has to be traced to those times when the so called Orthodox Vlachs, that is the Serbs, under pressure from the Turks in sixteenth and seventeenth centuries started to settle in Croatian regions" (see M. Artuković, *Towards the Roots of the Croatian-Serbian Conflict,* in *Croats and the Minorities in Croatia: Modern identities – the fourth Croatian Symposium on Teaching History,* Zagreb, 2014).

How to normalize relations with Serbia and the Serbian national minoritiy in Croatia on the basis of centuries-long "genesis of genocidal actions against Serbia in Croatia"? By Croatian self-deceit? The betrayal of national interests? The destruction of their own state? Committing hara-kiri? Praljak's little poison bottle? Ritual suicides of Croatian veterans? Emigration? Expelling? Crawling to Vučić? By sending representatives of associations that emerged in the Homeland War to resolve open issues between the two states with the Chetnik president of Serbia in Belgrade? Serbia considers those representatives to be the representatives of a genocidal nation, whom any Serb has the right to kill "like a dog by a fence" (Milan Paroški).

As long as the Serbs in Croatia are the lengthened arm of Belgrade, and the Croats are the lengthened arm of the foreign centers of power, neither a true reconciliation on the internal plan, nor the normalization on the bilateral plan can be expected. Such development of the situation will not rescind Serbia's entry into the European Union. The entry itself does not solve anything (if during the negotiations with Serbia, Croatia does not take a firm stand in the EU as a sovereign state), as we experienced during Croatia's entry in the EU. All the problems before entering the EU, even those in relation to local Serbs and neighbouring Serbia, remained problematic after the entry into the EU. Many problems, such as extinction, emigration, unemployment and demographic collapse,

A century of Serbian terror 1918 - 2018

have deepened, which only favours yesterday's aggressors, because the worse the situation in Croatia, the better for them. Why? Because Croatia does not exist.

The crisis of truth in Croatian-Serbian relations in Croatia cannot be swept under the rug any longer because it opens other crises: the crisis of further distrust in the Croatian Government and institutions, the crisis of trust, and it opens the crisis of the divided majority, the bearers of sovereignty. The crisis of truth suits Belgrade and its secret agents in Croatia. Serbia permanently produces the crisis of truth. Croatia pretends to be inexperienced in that, and it does not respond with all the available diplomatic tools. Croatia also does not use its membership in NATO and the European Union to suppress the production of the crisis of truth. On the contrary, Croatia makes certain moves on the internal plan, which favour Serbia's production of the crisis of truth.

So far, Pupovac has arbitrated from a high level. Now, ignoring the Constitution, he already co-creates. While, in fact, his views have remained in the eighties of the last century, when the Greater Serbian aggression was being created and encouraged. That procedure is now renewed in Croatia, because Croatian parties and politicians have not been constructing their politics towards the Serbian national minority and the Serbian state on truth for almost two decades, but on dreadful compromises that are only harmful for the state and the nation. By all indications, Zagreb is again becoming the political centre of Serbs in the Western Balkans, just as it was during the last phase in the existence of the Austro-Hungarian state, when the "annexing" was in fact being prepared with open help from the Serbian Independent Party, the hidden help of the National Party and of Belgrade agents.

In the current phase of the renewal of Greater Serbia, that is, the renewal of former relations on the territory of the former states of Yugoslavia, the Serbs in the "homeland" and the "scattered" Serbs at this moment need nothing more. The next more serious phase will be activated after Serbia's entry into the European Union. Until then Vučić will be handing to Grabar-Kitarović folder by folder (about the missing persons in Serbian camps) and he will be receiving in his den the delegations of grieved Croats who will be sent from Pantovčak at one time, and from the St. Mark's Square [the Government quarters] at another time. He will also be sending his aggrieved ones to them; whose number increases as the war is further behind us. Why? Because the balance of the guilt was accepted as the starting point of the politics of small steps and pushed into "humanitarian issues", which is the classic error in the steps of handling state politics. Had France and Germany tried to solve their open issues after World War II that way, they would not have solved them to this day.

The crisis of truth could become a permanent state of lies by the time of Serbia's entry into the European Union, if Croatia does not face it with the necessary seriousness and determination, as a sovereign state, an equal member of the European Union and a victim of the Greater Serbian aggression, that does not abandon its national interests, national security and international rights. With the existing Government and the opposition, Croatia is unfortunately incapable of such a turnaround at this moment. Objectively speaking, the Government and the opposition do not have the intellectual, moral, ethical or even political capacity for such an upright stance. Subjectively speaking, though, the situation is even worse.

(hkv.hr, 24 February 2018)

From ZO through SAO and RSK to URS, and again to ZVO...

The Serbian National Council, manipulating ("combining") the minority and national rights, like the historical and ethical rights in the past, passed the Declaration on the Rights of Serbs in Croatia on 13 February 2018. The Declaration was preceded by the project of the Political Science Academy of the Serbian National Council [SNV] – *The Future of Serbs in Croatia.* This project was presented to President Grabar-Kitarović and President Vučić in the presence of the Metropolite Porfirije, Dejan Jović and Milorad Pupovac. The report on the problems and perspectives of the Serbian community in Croatia was written by Prof Dejan Jović, President of the Council of Political Science Academy of the SNV, and former advisor of [Croatian] President Ivo Josipović. It should be read.

The Declaration on the Rights of Serbs in Croatia was passed at the meeting of the bloated SNV assembly on 13 February 2018 in the Zagreb Lisinski Concert Hall, a place of significance for the modern Croatian state, in the presence of Serbian President Vučić and Croatian President Grabar-Kitarović. In that Hall, on 25 February 1990, Dr Franjo Tuđman brought together the homeland and the exiled Croatia for the First General Parliament of the Croatian Democratic Union [HDZ] and started the democratic changes, national liberation and the renewal of the Croatian state. The HDZ was then the "Party of Dangerous intentions" [according to SD Party president I. Račan], and a characteristic title at the time was – "Who let the Ustasha come to Zagreb?". Today the situation is similar, we are faced with a rise in leftist and Chetnik extremism, but the HDZ is no longer dangerous for them.

The Declaration on the Rights of Serbs in Croatia arranged in 13 clauses, states among other things: "The institutions of the Serbian community, especially the Serbian National Council [SNV] and the Joint Council of Municipalities [ZVO - Zajedničko vijeće općina], must obtain minority self-government status, in accordance with their special founder sources – documents of international character, the Erdut Agreement and the Letter of Intentions".

The President of the Croatian Parliament, the Prime Minister and the President of the Republic did not state their positions about the Declaration, nor did the ruling coalition and the political parties. Unlike the nodding politicians, the professionals did react. Dr Mato Palić: "The mentioned claim that such status must be obtained because it derives from documents of international character is simply incorrect. None of the international agreements that regulate issues relating to the achievement of rights by the members of national minorities mentions special municipalities or other territorial units that would be organized according to ethnic principle. Something like that would be contrary to our Constitution. It is out of place to mention the Erdut Agreement, which has not been in force for many years".

A public Statement by the SNV and ZVO followed immediately, in which they complain about a "witch hunt". They say in the Statement – "it was requested that the 1998 decision of the Government of the Republic of Croatia and the 2010 conclusion of the Croatian Parliament related to

ZVO are implemented. It was also requested to implement the Program of this Government, which in its clause 10.3 foresees the manner in which to regulate the status of the Serbian National Council and other minorities' Councils in the Republic of Croatia".

Since the President did not get involved, the vice-President of the Parliament Furio Radin did. He replied to HINA's [Croatian national newspaper agency] question about the status of the Serbian minority self-government: "That is part of the Erdut Agreement. I am not afraid of any form of autonomy, or of any minority's self-government, to use the language of that Agreement. There are such minority self-governments for Croats and other minorities even in conservative Hungary, and nobody should be afraid of them. I am on the side of the minorities, when a minority community poses certain requests, it has my automatic solidarity". Radin's judgment lacks mostly, but not only, the historical contexts. If only a single dork was the problem! Let's find the contexts of the original goals in the documented heritage of "the Serbian community" in Croatia, embodied in the SNV, SDSS, SPC, Pupovac, Porfirije and Jović, and of course, in RSK Government Minister Stanimirović.

The last attempt to achieve Serbian autonomy in Croatia, including also the secession from Croatia, ended ingloriously with the great "historic" defeat. That defeat, considered as the criminal occupation of the justifiably established Republic of Serbian Krajina (RSK), has to be replaced step by step by victory in peacetime, as prescribed in Memorandum II. It is necessary, therefore, to remind the politicians and parties, especially those with the tendency to waddle into the fog, in love with brotherhood and unity, of the workflow of the most relevant Serbian historical sources in reference to the autonomy of the "Serbian community in Croatia". Those sources that are conspicuously avoided by Dejan Jović, Porfirije and Pupovac, and also the Great Assembly with its Declaration, and which were not mentioned at all in Vučić's two-day pilgrimage to the western areas of the Greater Serbia in Croatia. By invitation of the President of the Croatian state.

On 27 June 1990, the Municipal Assembly of Knin issued the Decision on the Establishment and Constituting Joint Municipalities of Northern Dalmatia and Lika – for the "government and management of the Municipal Community". "Milan Babić", signed it.

On 25 July 1990, the Serbian Parliament in the town of Srb, "starting from the universal principle of the right of a people to self-determination, including also the right to secession" issued and published the Declaration of Sovereignty and Autonomy of Serbian people. The Declaration begins with the following: "The Serbian people in the Socialist Republic of Croatia have the right to opt, together with Croatian people or independently, for the federative or confederative state organization in the establishment of new relations in Yugoslavia. The new form of the Yugoslav community cannot be chosen without the participation of the Serbian people in Croatia, which is especially valid in situations of legitimate secession. Nations secede, not states". Is the same rule valid for the Western Balkans region in the European Union? Of course.

On 30 September 1990, the Serbian National Council in Croatia "declared Serbian autonomy on ethnic and historical territories in which these people live, and which are located within the current borders of the Republic of Croatia as a Federative unit of the SFRJ". The autonomy was declared on the basis of the Declaration of Sovereignty and Autonomy of Serbian people and on the results of "declaring". In Croatia 567,731 Serbs declared their view. Out of that, 567,127 Serbs declared in favor and 144 Serbs voted against Serbian autonomy. There were 46 void votes.

On 21 December 1990, the Presidency of the Joint Municipalities of Northern Dalmatia and Lika adopted the Statute of the Serbian Autonomous Region [SAO] of Krajina. The SAO Krajina "is being established in order to achieve national equality, as well as specific cultural and historical characteristics of Serbian people living in the historical territories of Dalmatia and Vojna Krajina".

On 26 February 1991, the National Council of Serbian people of Slavonia, Baranja and West Srijem issued the Declaration of Sovereign Autonomy of Serbian people of Slavonia, Baranja and West Srijem. Clause 10 of the Declaration states: "The sovereign Serbian autonomy of Slavonia, Baranja and West Srijem exists and operates within the system of the current Republic of Croatia only under the condition that Yugoslavia exists as a federal state. In case such Yugoslavia ceases to exist or is transformed into a group of independent states, this autonomy will continue to exist as part of the parent state of Serbian people". If that Yugoslavia is renamed into these Western Balkans, the same rules apply.

On 29 February 1991, the Serbian National Council and the Executive Council of Serbian Autonomous Region of Krajina issued the resolution on the disassociation of the Republic of Croatia and Serbian Autonomous Region of Krajina. The Assembly of the Knin Municipality functioning as part of the Assembly of the SAO Krajina, on 18 March 1991 issued the Decision on Separation from the Republic of Croatia.

By the way, among the numerous documents of "the Serbian community in Croatia", let us also mention the Decision on the Affiliation of the Territorial Defense of the Serbian Region of Slavonia, Baranja and West Srijem to the armed forces of the SFRJ of 9 October 1991. There are also the Conclusions of the Great National Assembly of Slavonia, Baranja and West Srijem of 24 October 1991, where the Presidency of Yugoslavia and the Federal Secretary of National Defense are fully supported, Serbia is required to mobilize "within forty-eight hours" all males "in the age from 20 to 55" who are "capable of fighting and have escaped the areas affected by war", and the Declaration of the Unification with the SAO Krajina and Bosnian Krajina is adopted.

That is how the Belgrade brave men toyed with the "Serbian community in Croatia", all through 1995. Then, on 20 May 1995, the Assembly of the Republic of Serbian Krajina (RSK) issued the Decision on the Approach to the Realisation of Unification of the Republic of Serbian Krajina and the Republic of Serbia. On 29 May 1995, it adopted the Decision about the previous consent of the Assembly of the Republic of Serbian Krajina on the unification of the Republic of Serbian Krajina and the Republic of Serbia. The preliminary draft of the Law of United Republic of Serbia was also adopted. In the form of working material, the Decision on state unification of the Republic of Serbian Krajina and the Republic of Serbia is also known, which contains four clauses written on a Cyrillic typing machine (due to collective rout the Decision was not issued, author's comment). The new parastate would have been named the United Republic of Serbia.

And what happened? Croatia flashed [Operation Flash - *Bljesak*] in May, and then in August it blew a storm [Operation Storm - *Oluja*] and the ZO, SAO, RSK, municipalities, regions, krajinas, declarations, territorial defense, JNA, the Chetniks... all went into a hundred pieces, with the cry – "Let's run, brothers, victory is ours". Even Milošević himself soon ridiculed their defeat and the collective rout.

However, once "the hundred pieces" of the general "scattering" realized that for already four years the government in Croatia behaved in the old-Yugoslav way, that the HDZ Party was no longer the "party of dangerous intentions", on 26 February 2005 they held an RSK Renewal Assembly. There a Resolution was issued which claims that the RSK was an "autonomous political and legal subject carrying out the effective government on its territory until the brutal aggression by the Republic of Croatia that happened on 5 August 1995". In conclusion: "the Assembly of the Republic of Serbian Krajina requires that its declared protectors, the United Nations and the European Union, engage in the procedures of a democratic political process to solve the Serbian national issue of Serbian people in Croatia, and the process of solving the status of the Republic of Serbian Krajina".

Simultaneously with holding the RSK Renewal Assembly, the Serbian Radical Party adopted the Memorandum on the legal-political impossibility for the occupation of the Republic of Serbian Krajina to survive. The theses were: The Croats prepared for almost 50 years for the 'prolonged crime' on the Serbs and their ultimate removal from their century-long ancestral homes"; "the occupation of the Republic of Serbian Krajina was carried out in two phases"; "the idea of the political continuity of the Republic of Serbian Krajina is political realism. The only way for the normalization of future relations of Serbs and Croats is the cessation of the occupation of the Republic of Serbian Krajina and the final Serbian-Croatian demarcation". Furthermore: "Crimes and genocide must not be the basis for the creation of a serious European state. Thus, Croatia must not be rewarded for its criminal politics of killing and expelling of Serbs, but it must be forced by rational measures to accept the existence of the Serbian state within the borders of the Republic of Serbian Krajina".

The RSK Renewal Assembly, which grew into the Community of Municipalities – the equivalent of the Joint Council of Municipalities, was held in Belgrade at the time when HDZ and SDSS Party (of war criminal Goran Hadžić), Sanader and Pupovac were in the government, and Mesić was the President of the state. The Great Assembly of the Serbian National Council was held in February 2018, when the HDZ and SDSS, Plenković and Pupovac were in the government again, and

Kolinda Grabar-Kitarović was the President of the Republic. Pupovac is a constant. He almost succeeded to reach the territorial core, the unconstitutional ZVO, during the governance of J. Kosor (HDZ).

And now in 2018, when the SDSS and SNV converted in the meantime into a shelter for the defeated and a nursery for future defeats of the Serbian national minority gathered around them, in synergy with the SPC and Serbia, they are again causing fear and endangering the "Serbian community" in Croatia, like they did before the establishment of the Joint Council of Municipalities in 1990. The fear and endangering will stop if their request for the establishment of the ZVO is satisfied. But only until a new request is defined. It should be emphasized here that the Serbs in Croatia, under the leadership of Pupovac, did not apologize to the Croatian people for their participation in the aggression on Croatia. The aggression does not exist. They reject the official commemorations in Vukovar and the marking of Victory Day and Homeland Thanksgiving in Knin. They did not repent for the establishment of the parastates of ZO, SAO, RSK and URS. They are renewing myths wherever they go, myths of their innate anti-fascism to the innate Croatian genocidal character.

Pupovac's community did not do anything, not a single sign of reconciliation in truth, but they ask for everything, even the impossible – the status of political people with the right to secession, a self-governing territory, employment according to the national criterion, solving of community issues according to a privileged criterion… On the other hand, the Serbs in Croatia who accept both the status of national minority and the Croatian state as their Homeland, are experiencing the same Calvary as the Croatian veterans. True, they ask for the minimum – dignity. The Croatian state, governed by incompetents, centre-mists, inclusivists and other "ists" - or those queueing for their next mandate, at this moment cannot, does not, and even if it wanted to, would not know how to give this minimum, just as is the case with the majority of loyal citizens. Instead, they give "automatic solidarity" to the crisis of truth politics, of feigned endangering, production of myths and the reconstruction of unconstitutional and already previously defeated platforms.

(hkv.hr, 27 February 2018)

A century of Serbian terror 1918 - 2018

Eurovučić is a London, Brussels, Plebeians and Berlin project

When President Grabar-Kitarović emphasized in February 2018 that she spoke in Zagreb with the "European Vučić", and not with the Vučić from Glina (the Chetnik), she caused salvos of disapproval from the ranks of Croatian common sense. However, one has to be honest and say that "European Vučić" is not her fabrication, but adopted homework. She repeated what had been cooked before in Great Britain, accepted in Brussels and given to Berlin to carry out operationally.

The visit obtained a passing grade abroad as soon as the magic formula – "European Vučić' was pronounced. The politics implemented in Croatia since 2000 were just invoking, not to say preparing, the internal platform for the installation of the "European Vučić" project.

The Chetnik's retouched picture was pushed onto the European and world public space in September 2016 by the British journal *The Economist*, who wrote panegyrics to Vučić. Previously, in 2015, Vučić had hired former British Premier Blair as adviser. A year later, in 2016 he became the "European Vučić". Two years later, in 2018, the formula of the European Vučić concept was accepted by official Croatia too. Perhaps it was time to end the procrastination with the new Serbian order in the Western Balkans.

Blair's task was to bring the goals of Memorandum II to European level: to remove responsibility from Serbia for the aggression committed, to spruce up the Chetniks responsible for a full palette of crimes and make them fit the European "inclusive" format, to ensure Serbian superiority in relation to other states in the "territories of former Yugoslavia", and to bring Serbia closer to the negotiating position for membership in the European Union.

Blair was hired at the time when two Chetniks were in the positions of president of the state and head of the government, Tomislav Nikolić (Gravedigger) and Aleksandar Vučić (of Glina). Both are from Vojislav Šešelj's Serbian Radical Party, but "transformed" into the Serbian Progressive Party. All of this at the time when Serbia already had installed and established unquestionable, untouchable agents spread partly in the conquered, partly in the unconquered Western parts of the Greater Serbia in Bosnia and Herzegovina and in Croatia.

Despite not offering any proper arguments, the article in *The Economist* leaves no doubt as to its propagandist corroboration of Vučić's Europeanism. A typical sentence: "As a Europhile, former ultranationalist Aleksandar Vučić is the biggest surprise to Europe". And this is an "argument": "Western officers consider Mr. Vučić, according to the words of Sebastian Kurz, Austrian Minister of Foreign Affairs, the 'anchor of stability' in that region".

Why the "anchor of stability" in the region is not represented by a Croatian politician among all those many stokers of locomotives of the Western Balkans, is a separate topic for analysis of the post-Tuđman's politics. However, a healthy reminder is that until 2000 Croatia was the regional force and the guarantor of peace and stability in south-eastern Europe. Today it repeats parrot-fashion somebody else's empty phrases, such as this one on "European Vučić".

Croatia actually invited a certified European Chetnik to visit. But that is not all! Croatia also invited a European plebeian. At the end of November 2016, while Vučić was still head of the Serbian government, the Serbian Progressive Party became an associate member of the European People's Party. Vučić is undoubtedly a European project. The HDZ was bravely restrained in the entry voting. Approximately like Bakarić's SKH on Tito's SKJ congresses.

Vučić is today a European hope, just as Slobodan Milošević was a European hope at the beginning of the nineties. Europe allowed him to solve the "Yugoslav crisis" with fire and sword. Great Britain favored him by advocating for the embargo on imports of armaments. But what are the European Union and the United Kingdom prepared to invest in the "European Vučić" program in detriment of Croatia – that is, "a strong Serbia in the Balkans"? The Z4 plan? The "bigger Municipality" community? An independent RSK, or an RSK united with the Republic of Serbia?

Belgrade entertains itself from a distance by managing its position between the European Union and Russia. What about Croatia? Would the official [Croatia], unlike the Croatian Croatia, accept to give Serbia a state within its own state, so that Belgrade would become a member of the European Union, so that Serbia would get over Kosovo more

A century of Serbian terror 1918 - 2018

easily, and the Union would "kidnap" Serbia from the Russian embrace? If it submissively follows the British-Brussels hoax with the "European Vučić", then it should be aware of the axiom of British permanent politics – a strong Serbia is the guarantor of stability in the Balkans, "the end" and "amin". Both the monarchist and communist Yugoslavia have shown what is included in the "strong Serbia" package. Serbia was strong only within the various Yugoslavian states. And as strong as the other republics were weak.

A strong Serbia in the Balkans includes also its patronage over Croatia. That is where Vučić's message sent during his visit to Croatia comes from, about the fact that without doubt, he keeps Pupovac on a chain. And it is also known that Pupovac keeps Plenković's inclusive government on a short chain. That new Serbian order in the Balkans is also where the message, handed over in three file folders, comes from about the Croats killed in Serbia, about whom Croatia already had information.

With that message adjusted not to Europeanism but to Chetnik soullessness, the President of Croatia's only (atrocious) argument was entirely swept away, together with her authority, about a justified invitation to, as we later learned – the "European Vučić" – in fact an adapted Milošević. She said, in fact, that she would consider the invitation justified if during the visit Vučić revealed any piece of information about the missing persons in Serbia. He did not reveal any information, but he remained the "European Vučić". The European Vučić is the new dogma of the Western Balkans strategy. The stokers of the Western Balkans locomotive must not question it. They must implement it at any cost. And it costs more than it looks at first glance.

During the two-day parade in Croatia, flavored with unprecedented Serbo-Balkanic populism, the "European Vučić" of London, Brussels and Berlin, introduced himself as an ordinary Serbian Chetnik with a European certificate. He perceives Croatia as permanent prey of the Greater Serbian "moment". While it was evident that Croatia does not have its own established politics towards Serbia, founded on national interests and international law. By implementing someone else's politics, they impose aggression on our common sense with the idea of Chetniks actually being Europeans and the Croats their springboard.

When someone "from the territory of former Yugoslavia" obtains a European certificate, then he can do whatever he wants. Or does not want to. But only within the framework of "the territory of former Yugoslavia" south of [the river] Sutla. Already in Slovenia the political range of the "European Vučić" is not worth a bean. Let alone in Hungary, Bulgaria… the Eurovučićism (or the Eurochetnikism, if you like) has a limited and strongly defined space, which is critically concentrated on the Croatian state.

The lack of our own politics including national interests and national safety, is the consequence of the 3 January rupture of Croatian strategic partnership with the U.S.A. and the strategic leaning towards London, performed simultaneously with Račan's internal vengeance. The situation can still be saved (with more difficulty as time passes), before the formal disintegration of the Republic of Croatia happens according to the principles of a "strong Serbia". However, for an upright stance, among other things, one needs to have both the brain and the balls. The brain of our democratic legitimacies is contaminated with pro-Yugoslav populism of the lowest kind (let's forget about the past and turn to the future), whereas poultry farms with the production of eggs [also balls in Croatian] sent that same brain to ruin in a programmed way. That is why we do not have outstanding Croatian politicians and parties.

As far as Croatian Croatia is concerned, the "European Vučić" is a modern version of the logic of Yugoslav radical Vladimir Čerin – Belgrade soul and brain must be imposed on Zagreb by force. That is exactly what it means to impose "European Vučić" on Croats today. The local stokers of a "strong Serbia in the Balkans" are not justified by the fact that, London and Brussels and the "European plebeian family", as well yesterday's "fascist Germany" according to Serbs, are smirking behind the Chetniks.

The key question of who the U.S.A. will support remains open. It is difficult to expect that they will stand by someone with another's brain and soul and without his own balls.

(hkv.hr, 3 March 2018.)

A century of Serbian terror 1918 - 2018

The Chetnik quality of Vučić's Europeanism

When the ideologists and manipulators of the Euro-ideology renamed Chetnik Aleksandar Vučić the "European Vučić", they had to use criteria which undoubtedly led them to the conclusion that the Serbian Chetnik was a European prize. What standards did they use? By all indications it is a matter of previous acceptance of colourful lies, accepted especially in Croatia, with which, due to the nature of things, also the "European Vučić" was taken in. He was invented primarily for Croatian use.

Under the direction of 3 January politics, Croatia has, in fact, swallowed several cheap tricks intended towards her acceptance of the redefinition of the established state, and the renewed establishment of the Serbian order in the specific area of the "territory of former Yugoslavia". The first trick was extremely silly - Croatia is the locomotive of the Western Balkans. That is to say, Croatia is a springboard for Serbia and possibly for Bosnia and Herzegovina. Second trick: There is no homework that Croatia would not do. The third one is an incredible lie: Serbia's entry into the European Union is in Croatian strategic interest. Now there appears a fourth station of this Way of the Cross: Chetnik Vučić is European Vučić. To whom? To the stokers of the locomotive of the Western Balkans, to homework nerds, to Serbian lobbyists in Croatian politics and in false Europe.

All four tricks in fact form a system. It is the system of renewal of relations, which led to the aggression by Serbia, Montenegro and the rebelled Serbs. The system was handed over to students with democratic legitimacy to be consistently implemented in Croatia. Now that it has been implemented, it is clear that Croatia is mentally, politically and problematically returned to the state prior to the democratic changes. Had it not [been put back], then Plenković's useless Committee would discuss and adopt the recommendations also about the cockade, that totalitarian symbol, but also about the totalitarian Greater Serbian regime established in the occupied areas of Croatia. It lasted longer than the NDH!

The attempt to illuminate the "credibility" of the "European Vučić" tag seems futile. I would not deal with this futile business, had the "European Vučić" not entered the official vocabulary of Croatian politics at the highest level, like the cherry on the cake of Euro-nebulosity served so far. In view of the fact that the "European Vučić" as far as the basic values and political goals are concerned is the same as the "European Milošević", I consider the effort to be both good entertainment and a citizen's duty for a European person, a peasant without sewage – and who is not a Serb. That is why I observe the imposed tag through the prism of a true and false Europe, whose differences are explained in the Paris Charter published at the end of 2017. In hope that the consequences and the latest Euro-fallacies presented to us might be avoided, which undoubtedly requires that Croatian Europeans reject their European common sense, such as Kusić's "document"[42] about the false "confrontation with undemocratic regimes", which I have already thrown into the bin.

The imposed Euro ideological construct "European Vučić" must not be accepted, affirmed, or approved tacitly by European Croatia. Croatia must reject it with contempt and explain to the true and false Europe why it rejects it and why it despises it. The explanation, together with pertaining active politics, is not in an unachievable category, especially when based on historical truth, international law and national interests. Such an approach requires responsible and free persons, tireless, truth-loving Croats and brave Europeans. We have such persons, but not in politics, where Croatia and Europe need them the most. If we had them, we would oppose the current mass produced Euroairheads and also the "European Vučić". We would then not stoke the locomotive, or study the lessons mechanically, or invent strategic interests to Croatia's detriment.

The first question is simple: does Europe belong to Serbian President Aleksandar Vučić and does he, with Serbia, belong to Europe? The history of art does not testify this to any extent. Nor does the entire Serbian national history. Vučić's personal political history testifies that he does not have common points with the true Europe either. For centuries

---

42 Academician Zvonko Kusić, president of the Committee for Dealing with the Consequences of the Rule of Undemocratic Regimes, presented two Documents with the conclusions of the Committee in February 2018, in which the salute 'Ready for the Homeland' was deemed unconstitutional due to its connection with the NDH. The five-pointed red star, despite its connection with mass exterminations and breach of human rights, was not deemed unconstitutional due to its anti-fascist symbolism.

                    A century of Serbian terror 1918 - 2018

Serbia has lived outside the European civilization, without contact with whole periods of European culture. Serbia and Vučić can replace the European culture, as history has shown, with a non-European civilization and culture, without any feeling of loss. From the historical and cultural aspect, the "European Vučić" does not pass elementary scrutiny.

However, if Europe accepts the "European Vučić" tag, then it threatens itself, especially in the region of the Republic of Croatia. False Europe is not true Europe. By pushing the "European Vučić" tag it showed its flaws from the past, when it accepted Chetnik Vučić in the function of "European Milošević", but its prejudices relate to the future, when it tries to build the future of the Western Balkans with a Chetnik. Because of that: "its advocates are orphans of their own choice" since they know very well that the goal of Serbia is a breakthrough to the West. Chetnik Vučić was to realize that breakthrough. Since he did not realize it, now it's the "European Vučić's" turn.

The false Europe, founded on false assumptions and self-deceit, on forgeries and misconceptions, cannot be a community of equal people. With his "Euro jackpot" prize, Vučić became the favoured politician of the Western Balkans. The Western Balkans is also a fabrication of false Europe, because it is nobody's native country, or homeland, not even an internationally legal subject. It does not exist, just like the "European Vučić".

The authors of the "European Vučić" "are fascinated with the empty belief in unstoppable progress" of the Western Balkans. What type of progress can be expected when a Chetnik is placed on the European pedestal? A backwards progress. Or the continuation of a circular course of history of Serbian order in the territory of South-eastern Europe. That means that the creators of the tag are "steeped in prejudices, superstitions and ignorance, dazzled by empty, obtrusive visions of a utopian future, they reflexively suffocate any different opinion".

Then, whoever does not think that the Chetnik Movement is European is in for trouble. Whoever does not think that Croatia is a locomotive, he is already written off. Whoever does not want to do the homework, is also written off. And who does not think that Serbia's entry into the European Union is a Croatian strategic goal, he is a traitor of the false Europe, of real Yugoslavianism and Serbian antifascism with the pertaining Chetnik Movement. The European Vučić, just like the Chetnik Vučić, has never betrayed the idea of a Greater Serbia. He would not have become the "European Vučić" had he betrayed it.

In which joint project of the true Europe did Serbia and Aleksandar Vučić participate? Not in a single one. As far as the false Europe is concerned, Serbia participated, at the time with Vučić's ideological fathers, in the dismembering of Croatia through the joint project with fascist Italy. Serbia also participated with Vučić in the false Europe's project, with which it tried to preserve communist Yugoslavia under Belgrade's boot. The "European Vučić" label is part of the continuity in the relation between the false Europe with Greater Serbia.

Serbia never accepted the European ideal of solidarity towards Europe, therefore also towards Croatia, not even in Vučić's time, then as in now. On the contrary, it was always un-solidary and supported denationalized regimes, parties and politicians. During the nineties Vučić accepted to be a player for the false Europe, which gave a free hand to Belgrade to destroy Croatia, under the condition that the destruction was fast and efficient. Therefore, even as a Chetnik, Vučić carried out the European politics of the false Europe.

"European Vučić" is the president of the Serbian Progressive Party. However, the European "spirit of progress was born out of love and loyalty toward our native states" and not out of love toward the imperialism of the "homeland". The "European Vučić" is advanced in the backward ideas of Vuk S. Karadžić, Ilija Garašanin… all the way to Slobodan Milošević and Vojislav Šešelj. It is on their ideas, and not those of the Fathers of Europe, that the Serbian politics are based. It is impossible to build the idea of European cultural unity (in diversity) on them, whether or not Vučić is called European, Chetnik, Byzantine or Greater Serbian.

The European spirit of unity involves the assumption of responsibility for the future of European societies. The Croatian is a European society. But, with embedded viruses of communism (now anti-fascism) and Greater Serbianism it can be integrated into a Western Balkans society that even today cannot exist without the Euro-Chetnik Movement and documents such as the one offered to us by Plenković's Committee headed by the

A century of Serbian terror 1918 - 2018

cheaply bought academician Kusić. There is no embedded European spirit of unity between Croatia and Serbia, except that the JAZU/HAZU academician Dušan Džamonja was also a member of SANU, and Dr Vojislav Šešelj was also a member of the Croatian Philosophical Society. That spirit can be imposed on Croatia only by force. Forcing Croatia is the Chetniks' pretense of the spirit of unity. It is a half-hearted renewal of the communist brotherhood and unity.

True Europe is a community of nations and states. Chetnik Vučić, however, considers Croatia to be a state of Serbian people. Only the false Europe and its servants know when and where he changed his opinion to such a degree that he became the "European Vučić". True Europe is also "unity in diversity". On the occupied Croatian territory Vučić's progressive Republic of Serbian Krajina, backed by Serbia and the false Europe, expelled all European people different from Serbs. Then it expelled also the Serbs, because Serbs do not want to live in European Croatia. She is always to some degree fascist and genocidal, according to the criteria of the classic Chetnik Movement and according to the criteria of the Euro-Chetnik Movement. Because is not Serbian.

A true European citizen does not accept imposition and extortion of any kind. The "European Vučić" tag is imposed on the European citizens in Croatia and it ultimately requires them to renounce their love for the Homeland and citizen loyalty. The one who imposes a lie is equally dangerous to the European scale of values, as the one who invents it. The introduction of the "European Vučić" tag to Croatia is part of the already seen attempt to create political unity, the empire of single-mindedness. The collaboration of Great Britain and Greater Serbia in that regard is a long-lasting endeavor of the false Europe. London imposed the "European Vučić" tag even in the circumstances of the exit from the "European Union.

Croatian politicians must not appease false Europe if they want to be Croatian. Europe's future does not lie in the platitudes of the false Europe (and the false Croatia), which "enslaves our perceptions", while it undermines the European nations and common culture with "illusions and self-deception about what is European and what should be European". Croatian politicians should stop deluding themselves and the people. And oppose "that danger to our future". The "European Vučić" label is a danger for the Croatian nation. It is the duty of Croatian politicians to defend the Homeland from dangers. That makes them European. They will never become European by adopting the criteria of good stokers, nerds and notorious liars, but are turning into the Western Balkans norm, above which only the imposed and swotted lie about the "European Vučić" sticks out.

(hkv.hr, 6 March 2018)

Serbia and the SPC are building a new Greater Serbian myth – Operation Storm is a pogrom

In the broadcast of the "celebration" of Operation Storm in Bačka Palanka, Serbia (4 August 2018) a complete unity of views of Serbian politicians "in these territories" could be observed, and of the clergy of the Serbian Orthodox Church. Also, the absence of and the silence on the elementary facts which led to Storm and about Storm in general. Almost an hour and a half of Greater Serbian howling flavored with the pathos of a "cultural-artistic program" was played out under the state slogan "Storm is a pogrom". There was no mention at all about the relation between causes and consequences. It is now perfectly clear that the Greater Serbs are creating a new myth. A myth about Storm. It will continue only to be expanded from one year to the next. Until the "first rifle" of the endangered Serbs is fired again, and they are endangered everywhere except in Serbia, as it was heard.

What Irinej, Dodik and Vučić said does not need to be repeated. That is, it will be repeated in the anti-Croatian press in Croatia. Also, the parliamentary representative of the Serbian National Minority in the Croatian Parliament, the inclusive Milorad Pupovac, heard out the entire play. He did not speak. He went to Serbia to listen; he will speak in Croatia.

I am holding back from starting with Vučić's Palanka quotations. And then I remembered that the President of the Republic of Croatia only this year called him "European Vučić". The whole of Europe acknowledges and knows that Operation Storm is blameless. Only "European Vučić",

A century of Serbian terror 1918 - 2018

President of Serbia, does not know it. Thus, instead of quoting Vučić, I quote the President of Croatia.

I am also refraining from starting with quotations from Pupovac's *Novosti* newspaper, but then I remembered that he is the executive power, inclusive, in the inclusive anti-populist Government despite the electoral will. It would be absurd to quote the *Novosti* newspaper. I would actually be quoting the Government's views. I am only unclear which government is the right one, the one from Bačka Palanka or the one from Knin. Or both? If both are the right ones, then we are talking about the socialist Yugoslav Government of the SRH [Socialist Republic of Croatia].

The Bačka Palanka people's event revealed to *urbi et orbi* that Serbia "will no longer allow" any new Storms. They are, it seems, that sure that the continued pacification of Croatia will result in no resistance towards the Greater Serbia endeavour. The complete staging of the event is the exact opposite of the staging by Krešimir Dolenčić and the turning off the electricity[43] to the Croats! He prevented the people. The Serbian production in Bačka Palanka surpassed even Milošević's agitprop machine at the beginning of the nineties. This implies that Vučić is as European as Milošević.

What is the purpose of the Greater Serbian myths? To mobilize "all who are fit for fighting" onto tanks. Hence, in suitable circumstances they are also useful for the collapse of the Croatian state. Yet when in an equal fight they end up losing, then they order the evacuation "for all who are unfit fit for fighting" and all who are fit ("heavenly drama") on tractors. Then they turn the defeat into a new myth. That is the circular course of Greater Serbian self-delusion, of Yugoslav sympathizing and the Croatian fifth column that favors them. In the background there is Garašanin peering out with the thesis that the Croatian nation and the

---

43 In July 2018 at the concert staged by theatrical director Krešimir Dolenčić as part of the celebrations for the return of the Croatian football team from Russia, the electricity to the stage was cut off just at the point when the Croatian most popular patriotic singer Marko Perković Thomspon was about to sing the 'signature' tune *Geni kameni* – Stone Genes, which grew to become a symbol of the Homeland war and was a special request by the team captain Luka Modrić.

Croatian state do not exist. If they do exist, then they are criminal. The myths serve them as evidence for that. Serbia, the multiple aggressors, does not want to exit that circle.

However, what does Croatia want? If it thinks that by privileging Vučić's Pupovac it will stop the influence of Greater Serbian myths in Croatia, then it is mistaken. How does it intend to prevent the penetration of myths in Croatian media space? How to do it in the political environment? How to defend the Croatian Assembly when it is being converted into a training centre for Greater Serbians myths? Through inclusiveness? Privileging? Concealed Yugoslavism? Plentiful financing? All these forms have already been used up in the Socialist Republic of Croatia. They ultimately led to the Greater Serbian aggression, but during the last eighteen years they have been renewed and imposed again.

Should the Greater Serbian myths be ignored? The Jasenovac myth has also been ignored, and based on it the Chetnik Movement was mobilized and the uprising launched against the Croatian state. I do not doubt that the myth about Operation Storm will also serve the same purpose and goal when the time arrives - namely, that Croatia is put within the borders which Serbia allows. The message of the myth is – Krajina is not part of Croatia.

The first day of Operation Storm, 4th August, is the day when Serbia and the "Serbian states", those which Serbia did not yet "liberate" completely, commemorate the "Storm victims". On the afternoon of that day, the command was issued by the military and political top of the rebel Serbs to evacuate "all citizens unfit to fight". Serbia celebrates the defeat.

On the second day of Operation Storm, Croatia liberated Knin from the perennial terror of "all for fight" fit and unfit rebel citizens. On 5 August, Croatia celebrates its victory over the aggressor, the word that never crosses "Premier" Plenković's lips. However, it looks like Serbia won. Serbia officially turns the defeat into an anti-Croatian myth for the fourth year running. It also looks like Croatia lost the war against the aggressor, because it finances the producers of myths, it privileges the transmitters of myths and it does not have any "strategy" to respond to the anti-Croatian myths. Except for the false and empty mantras that the entry of Serbia (created on anti-Croatian myths) into the European Union – is of strategic interest to Croatia.

The harmless welcome of Croatian football players, the second-best team in the world, was declared by the current order as a soft Ustasha state strike. The meeting in Bačka Palanka, with the presence of Milorad Pupovac, was a tough Serbian strike on the Croatian state, its very foundations.

(hkv.hr, 7 August 2018)

Dačić brought the Slavist Congress under socialist Yugoslavia

The Sixteenth International Slavist Congress was held in Belgrade (20 - 27 August 2018). The Congress was organised by the International Slavist Committee, Federation of Serbian Slavist Associations, International Slavist Centre and the School of Philology of the University of Belgrade. It was held under the sponsorship of Aleksandar Vučić, President of Serbia, known in Croatia as a Chetnik, in recent time enforced as "European Vučić". About one thousand scientists from fourty-three countries attended the Congress. According to Serbian media "the Congress was to a large extent dedicated to the linguist Aleksandar Belić".

According to available Serbian information, it can be concluded that the Congress fell short of expectations, despite good organisation, high sponsorship and numerous participants. That was due to the fact that it did not explicitly emphasise that at the beginning of the world there was only the Serbian language, from which developed all other "varieties", more or less "artificially". Therefore, in order to avoid further "complications", the Serbian Foreign Affairs Minister had to intervene at the end of the Congress.

Thus, little Slobo [Slobodan, as in Milošević], Minister Ivica Dačić, took the Slavistic studies into his own hands, and told the gathered scientists that: "The situation in the Balkans territory is further complicated by the constant process of fragmentation of the Serbian language, where from a common and unified language corpus, the creation of new language varieties is justified for political and state-building reasons, and although these varieties are not different linguistically, on a political level they obtain different, national state characteristics and very frequently build their identity by denying their original language".

Dačić is a political scientist of Greater Serbian orientation, he is not a linguist. The Congress participants were scientists, to whom he nevertheless gave a lesson from the imperialist programme "Serbs are all and everywhere" of Vuk Stefanović Karadžić. When a head of the Socialist party speaks about the "fragmentation" of the Serbian language, he thinks of the "fragmentation" of the Social Federative Republic of Yugoslavia - SFRY, conceived as a screen for Greater Serbia. And since Croatian is a fragmented part of the Serbian language, Croatia is also a "piece" of Serbia. That is his "scientism". The implication is that Croats do not have their own identity, therefore, their language, nor do they have the right to a state. Whatever they have in that regard, originates from the Serbs. The Croatian language, however, was created long time ago with all the functions a standard language must have.

Dačić showed himself up in front of the Slavists also with new notions about the fact that the U.S.A., in their fight for "independence from the British Empire" did not dispute "for one single minute" their "English language, without the pretension for it to become the American language, which led to the situation that even today the U.S.A., Great Britain, Canada, Australia and New Zealand, not only speak the same language, but look at the world and the developments in it with the same common views".

Dačić, Serbia is not Great Britain. The English language arrived in the above-mentioned countries in a different way, whereas Croatian and Serbian developed independently of each other. True, there were multiple endeavours to make one language out of the two. That was unsuccessful, just as it was not successful merging the two nations into one, or two states into one. The comparison with English does not work. English was transferred to other states. Croatian developed independently before the entry into an association with Serbia (in 1918). Therefore, Croatian is not a "fragment" of the Serbian language.

Dačić further also embarrassed himself in the continuation of his speech by repeating the thesis of Vuk Stefanović Karadžić in which he does not deny only languages, but entire nations too. In order to achieve a general (Yugoslav) dimension of the Serbian language, Dačić was photographed with the Congress participants under a poster on which the following was written in Cyrillic alphabet: "Socialist Yugoslavia". This can be seen in the photo attachments of the official page of the Ministry of Foreign Affairs, where the entire Dačić's speech was published.

Dačić's speech is actually a big scandal to which the Croatian institutions did not react. It represents an offense, a provocation, and the continuation of the Serbian aggression. We have received only the following information from the corresponding Croatian institutions: "Institutional scientists and members of the Terminological Commission of the International Slavist Committee, Dr sc Lana Hudeček, Dr sc Kristian Lewis and Dr sc Milica Mihaljević have participated in the Commission's session on 23 August 2018 in Belgrade. The Commission's meeting was held within the 16th International Slavist Congress (20 - 27 August). The members of the Terminological Commission have accepted the proposal of the scientists from the Institute that the next meeting of the ISC Terminological Commission would take place on 9 May 2019 in Zagreb. After the meeting the E-dictionaries and e-lexicography Scientific Congress will be held (10 and 11 May 2019)".

Dačić's nonsense language leads to Božo Maksimović Kundak Orthography manual of 1929 and similar Yugo-unitarist solutions of which we have had plenty during the past one hundred years of Serbian linguistic, political, diplomatic, judicial, gendarmerie and all other terrors. Serbian gendarmes would, in fact, become education ministers. Aleksandar Belić (1876 – 1960), to whom the Congress was "largely dedicated", was not a gendarme. However, he was the most significant ideologue of lingvo-unitarism in "socialist Yugoslavia", and even "before".

In the Kingdom of Serbs, Croats and Slovenes (SHS), especially after the Vidovdan Constitution declared the nonexistent "Serbian-Croatian-Slovene" as the official language, Serbian had become (even in Croatia) the official language in state administration, army, education, railways, newspaper agencies…The Cyrillic alphabet started to suppress the Latin alphabet. All that was reliably and "professionally" serviced by Aleksandar Belić with his Croatian "collaborators" and like-minded followers through the *Our language* journal. With that journal the Croatian language, and especially the lexical features, were declared provincial, dialectal, incorrect and redundant.

In communist Yugoslavia (Dačić's socialist Yugoslavia), Serbian was imposed in the army, administration and the *Tanjug* newspaper agency. "And then again an opinion poll…, then (again) under Belić's organizational and professional leadership and under strong political custody, a new agreement was reached (in Novi Sad, 1954), on the compulsory dual language name (Croatian-Serbian – Serbian-Croatian), and later a "common" Orthography was published (1960) …" (ac. Marko Samardžija, *Croatian? Yes, but Serbian!*, Zagreb, 2006).

Serbia takes advantage of every occasion to return "in full measure" to the Greater Serbian tracks by lubricating the unitarian axes of Vuk Stefanović Karadžić, the rifle butt of Monarchist Yugoslavia, the restoring Communist party of Yugoslavia (unimportant whether it's *grah* [beans in Croatian] or *pasulj* [beans in Serbian], as long as there is some), *Our Language* of Aleksandar Belić and the Serbian Academy of "Sciences and Arts".

The Croatian political and professional structures and institutions pretend not to see the renewal of the Greater Serbian theses that ultimately lead to a new war in the states which Serbia has not yet "liberated" from the unacceptable "fragmentation" and the introduction of the "varieties". They deal with the fragmentation of the Croatian society and state: with political stability, inclusiveness, the "school for life", false orthography, e-lexicography, experimental education, [use of] tablets and with their (altogether un-national) most important strategic goal – the entry of Serbia into the European Union, averting the attention of the Croatian people from the real and historically proven threats from the East. All that matters, as far as language is concerned, is that *komšije* [neighbours in Serbian] understand their neighbours, and that the neighbours [Croats] do not work out what *komšije* and their servants in Croatia are preparing for them.

(hkv.hr, 4 September 2018)

A century of Serbian terror 1918 - 2018

The Globus make-over of Chetnik Vuk Drašković

One of the tactical issues which the Greater Serbian Belgrade intelligentsia and their Croatian servants are constantly dealing with is how and at which point to implement a particular issue in the forced introduction of "Belgrade soul and brain" into Croatia. A practical example is exquisitely illustrated in the Vuk Drašković interview published in the journal *Globus* on 21 September 2018. Darko Hudelist remembered publishing his first interview with him in the magazine Start "in late summer 1989". That interview is a real treasure of Greater Serbian attempts in which Drašković offloaded as a specialist on Greater Serbia's borders. He was "transformed" in the meantime, so that the Serbian portal *koreni.rs* wrote about him already in 2016 - *How did a 'Chetnik' fall in love with NATO.*

The motive for the new conversation was reportedly Drašković's still unpublished novel, in which he admires King Aleksandar, who allegedly wanted to "make Yugoslavia into the America of the Balkans", with which the author's already previously sick imagination achieves a new dimension in lying. The Croatian public might be interested in novels by Austrian, Hungarian, Italian and Turkish writers, which all come from countries that have more or less invaded Croatia. Yet, according to the Yugoslav recipe of King Aleksandar and others, mainly Serbian novels are admitted into the modern Croatian public space. Drašković's novel, as can be concluded from the interview, is a contribution to the centenary of the occupation of "these areas" and a call for new ones.

The editorial treatment alone, in the technique of production of oblivion, introduced Drašković in the *Globus* journal as a "politician and writer who announced the Croatian – Serbian war". It is historically correct that Vuk Drašković intensified, invoked and encouraged Serbian military aggression on Croatia and Bosnia and Herzegovina, with his war-agitating rhetoric. He is one of the key architects of Serbian terror "in these areas", as a writer in the service of Greater Serbia's ideology and as a shifty politician.

In 1990, Drašković stated that all Yugoslav calamities originate from the Croats. In 1991, he confirmed the continuity of Greater Serbia's politics as his political program: "The optimal program is (…) the unification of all Serbian states into one country. An optimal program must also count on, for example, Skadar. (…) If the land is ours up to Ogulin, if that is written in the *Načertanije*, our goal will be to reach Ogulin at a time of suitable historical circumstances. (…) Now it is insane and unimaginable to insist on annexing Temišvar to Serbia. However, had Draža Mihailović won in 1945, we could have achieved it" (Political Magazine *Serbia*, special edition, Belgrade, 1991).

As can be seen from the quote, Drašković sticks firmly to the Greater Serbian axis Garašanin – Mihailović – SANU Memorandum, in which King Aleksandar is one of the more important semi-axles. His "optimal program" derives from Draža Mihailović' manifesto: "I will fight for the most sublime ideals a Serb can have: the liberation and unification forever of all Serbian states. (…) Wherever there are Serbian graves, that is a Serbian state". In fact, on the eve of the collapse of Yugoslavia, Drašković was the first to proclaim the King's Chetnik Mihailović "the first European guerrilla fighter".

In addition to *Načertanije*, Drašković's "optimal program" also includes messages published in major Greater Serbian works, such as *Serbian Krajina – Serbs in our north-western regions* (Zagreb, 1939), *Homogenous Serbia* (1941) by Stevan Moljević and *Serbs and Serbian states – the ethnographic problem of Serbian people* (1942) by Milutin Nedić. The source of the "optimal program" is recorded in the introduction to *Načertanije*: The basis of Serbian politics is that it tends to annex to itself all Serbian states that surround it, and not to limit Serbia to its current borders". The source was written, what a surprise, just at the time of the Karađorđević dynasty, Aleksandar's ancestors.

Since 1982, Vuk Drašković is a shaggy-bearded Chetnik with a tie, and until then he was a servant of the regime and a successful communist parasite. He was born in 1946 in Banat in a partisan family originally from eastern Herzegovina that occupied a house of expelled Germans. Since it was necessary to work in agriculture in Banat, the family returned to where they came from, living on the "heritage of our revolution". His father was captain of the JNA Army, who registered as his day of birth "29 November" (the day of the late Republic, but the exact day of birth of little Vuk remained unknown, same as that of Josip Broz). After graduating at the Law School in 1968, he immediately became a regime man employed at TANJUG, where he worked until 1977. During his last two years there he worked as a correspondent from Lusaka. He was returned home to the "fortress of socialist and non-aligned countries self-management" after he sent to the world the false information that Rhodesia had attacked Mozambique.

From 1977 to 1980, he is the head of Yugoslav Trade Unions information service. He joins the literary circles of the Greater Serbian propaganda, whether by order or personal choice immediately after the death of the Yugoslav Marshal with the novel *Knife* (1982). He then also joins the practical (Greater Serbian) politics. He is the founder of the SNO [Serbian National Renewal], and soon also of the SPO [Serbian Renewal Movement]. He promotes Greater Serbia created in peacetime, by sending Serbian volunteers to the battlefield. He simulates opposition to Milošević, his unattainable model, only to join Milošević in an alliance in 1944, which he terminated the following year, creating an illusion of Serbian democracy. In 1997 in Ravna Gora, he calls for the occupation of Knin and he offers himself to be at the front of the tank column. Based on the rhetoric of such pre-election period, he becomes the Vice-President of the Serbian Government in 1988, but is dismissed in 1999. In 2004, he becomes the Minister of Foreign Affairs of Serbia and Montenegro.

His political path as regime apparatchik portrays him as a classic convert and living proof of the small step between a hardcore communist and a possessed Chetnik. His novel *Knife*, though, reveals an author totally immersed in the production of overall 'Serbian endangering' in neighboring "lands", which because of that have to be "liberated" from Muslims and from Croats, and then "annexed", that is, occupied. Drašković was both a communist and an anti-communist. He was a fighter for peace, while lining up Chetnik volunteer hordes. He was an anti-Milošević, but used to state – "Milošević is a fighter for peace". In the middle of the last decade (2006), he played a pro-European politician with the main task of preventing Croatia's entry into the European Union.

Drašković is one of the key Serbian figures responsible for the psychological preparation of Serbs for aggressions on neighboring states and nations. During the preparation for the military aggression, he was the first, before his wedding best man Vojislav Šešelj, to dictate the western border of Serbia along the line Virovitica – Karlovac –

Karlobag. In building his "optimal program" he started with the Ustasha, of course, who are a synonym for Croats. Then he declared Jasenovac the largest Serbian underground city. The only salvation from Ustasha and Jasenovac he saw in the Greater Serbia. If there is no Yugoslavia (which in his interpretation was once broken by "Croatian secessionism", the second time by "Milošević"), he would say, the only alternative is Greater Serbia. For this reason, he was announcing the "unification of all Serbian states", starting with Macedonia all the way "up to the old Serbian port of Rijeka". That plan connects him intimately and practically with King Aleksandar.

After the occupation of Knin he stated that "the stories about Knin as a historical Croatian city are worthless, because with the departure of Knin Croatia will not be damaged in neither the cultural or spiritual regard", which coincides with Vučić's newest "historical" vomit about how the Croatian flag never fluttered in Knin before Operation Storm.

Even Milošević became fed up of him as a Serb blitherer. He arrested him twice. Once he even gave him a thorough beating. He survived two assassination attempts in internal Serbian turmoil. Despite that, as a Greater Serb "from the bottom of the pan", he tried to launder Milošević's responsibility in front of the international community. The aggression (the "war" as Vuk and *Globus* say) is not controversial, the Serbian military defeat is controversial. The goal is clear, it is necessary to wash away the responsibility from the Serbs and Serbia, so he says: "A curse will not befall the Serbs for causing the conflicts, but neither must the historical shame to have faced fascism on their knees". This statement was embedded in the goals of Memorandum II, which is also what a considerable part of the Croatian political and media mainstream conforms to. Because of this, investigations into Serbian crimes are being blocked in Croatia, and attempts intensified regarding the "common guilt for the war", which happened due to a "conglomerate of bad politics" (Ivo Josipović).

This person, Drašković, has however written a new novel of which he talks in the *Globus* journal glorifying King Aleksandar Karađorđević as the "greatest personality in Serb history" (and what about Saint Sava?) who wanted to make Yugoslavia become the America of the Balkans (madness!); the one who, had he not been killed in 1934, would have that

A century of Serbian terror 1918 - 2018

same year given "Banovina Croatia" to the Croats (as if); who understood that he made a mistake with the politics of the integral Yugoslavism (a construction); who did not want to accept the proclamation of Greater Serbia as a goal of the war, but the unification of Serbs, Croats and Slovenes into a common state (unification is occupation of "these areas"); who was congratulated by Wilson on the creation of Yugoslavia with the desire to create Yugoslavs (a sick imagination); who was allegedly desperate about the assassination of Croats in the Belgrade Parliament in 1928 (come on!), and so on, Drašković continues to mislead.

I agree with him in one thing: "Communist Yugoslavia was only a replica, while the 1918 Aleksandar's Yugoslavia was the original". Both of them were totalitarian, undoubtedly anti-Croatian and they both collapsed with the unsolved "national issue", claiming that they had solved it. However, I do not agree that Wilson congratulated Aleksandar on the occupation, since the Serbian "annexation" of Vojvodina, Croatia and Bosnia and Herzegovina was in 1918 in direct contradiction with Wilson's 14 clauses and the instruction about people's right to self-determination. The idea that Wilson requested Aleksandar to create the non-existent "Yugoslavs" belongs to the Guessing Magician journal, into which the *Globus* converted by building the affirmation path for Drašković's phantasies.

Let's remind ourselves that the Serbian expansionist program, Ilija Garašanin's *Načertanije*, was created during the Karađorđević dynasty. On the basis of that program, the Karađorđević's supported the 'Serbian rebellion in southern Hungary in 1848. By obtaining his elder brother's resignation, Aleksandar Karađorđević (1888-1934) was proclaimed heir to the throne in 1909, and regent in 1914. He took advantage of Russia's exit from the war to get the Montenegrin Assembly to expel his grandfather King Nikola I and decide to join Serbia on 16 November 1918.

When did he become "the greatest personality in Serb history"? While ignoring the demands of Croatian geese in the Belgrade fog, he proclaimed the Kingdom of Serbs, Croats and Slovenes on 1 December 1918, thereby imposing the dynasty and himself before the Constitutional Assembly's decision. He ruled the Kingdom for two and a half years without a Constitution. With the Vidovdan Constitution (1921), he called for elections, summoned and dissolved the National Assembly, proposed and rejected laws, and became Commanding Officer of the Army. Up to 1929, 21 out of the 23 governments stepped aside at his request. The novelist Vuk Drašković found those elements inspiring in glorifying Aleksandar and the "America of the Balkans".

Aleksandar considered the Kingdom ("the Balkan America") to be the extended Serbian national state, for which reason he rejected mainly Croatian proposals on federalisation and conducted a repressive and centralist internal politics. His role in the preparation of the assassination attempt on Croatian representatives in the Belgrade National Assembly (1928) has never been completely unravelled, yet it was undoubtedly an expression of the King's will and politics. After the attempt, he offered Croats a "peaceful separation" with the so-called amputation plan, according to which the Croats would remain without a great part of their territory, and the Serbs within the borders of the desired Greater Serbia. When this amputation according to a Greater Serbia map did not pass, he abolished the Constitution and citizens' rights and on 6 January 1929 practically undertook a *coup d'état* by introducing dictatorship, becoming the legislative and executive authority, while the judiciary functioned according to extraordinary laws.

Aleksandar's dictatorial system relied on Serbian generals, gendarmes, the army and the huge corrupted and Serbianised state machine. He forbade national names and symbols. He invented the Yugoslav nation – which Drašković attributes to the desire to replicate the U.S.A. On 3 October 1929, Aleksandar renamed the state into the Kingdom of Yugoslavia, dividing it territorially into nine Banovina. They were tailored with dictatorial scissors according to the goals of Greater Serbia. The Serbian majority was secured in six Banovina. His foreign policy was extremely harmful to Croatian interests. For example, Rijeka was left to Italy with the 1924 Rome agreements. The Central European and Mediterranean Croatia was further Balkanised in 1934 by his Balkan Pact (Yugoslavia, Romania, Turkey and Greece).

He was killed on 9 October 1934 in Marseille by Croatian and Macedonian national forces in the attempt of liberation from Greater Serbian dictatorship. Earlier, at the beginning of the year, he had established the Regency (Prince Pavle, Senator Stanković and Ban

Perović), which would rule the state in case of his death. Thus, we are talking about a classic dictator of Greater Serbian magnitude.

The Yugoslav political option, both left and right, as well as the Greater Serbian option, call King Aleksandar Karađorđević – the "Unifier". That unification together with the "annexation" (occupation), seems to be the key motive guiding Drašković in writing the novel about Aleksandar. That is, he estimated that at this moment it was not possible to go towards future "annexations" from the position of "the first guerrilla fighter of Europe", Chetnik Draža Mihailović, but that instead, it was necessary to go in a roundabout way through the Yugoslav 'fiddle bow', which the Croatian geese follow very well. That is why his novel about King Aleksandar is primarily intended as spiritual food for the Yugoslav left and right wings in Croatia. Should it achieve practical success, this novel will be a replica of *Knife*.

There simply is no other reason for the new Yugoslavisation and Croatian affirmation of the author and the novel. As a writer, Drašković is already proven to be literarily impotent but useful in the Greater Serbian way. All the rest related to the figure and the work, including his historical interpretations expressed in the interview, represents pure nonsense by a hard-core Chetnik longing for power, or at least public promotion, in order to freely disseminate "in these areas" his repeatedly failed theses, primarily the ultimatum – either the Yugoslav community or the Greater Serbia. With his new novel, he is offering the Croatian geese a return to "Yugoslavism".

Despite this, *Globus* has presented Drašković and the novel, which has not been published yet, nor is its title known, in the best light. The novel, *Globus* reports, has even before its publication "caused a huge interest among the Belgrade public, but also of more extensive public" (does a nomination for Nobel Prize follow?) and it is assumed that "it could be very interesting also to Croatian readers due to a series of reasons" (a wrong assumption). If for no other reason, because "Drašković has worked on it for about ten years, among other, as a true historical researcher, having read and analyzed several hundreds of documents (both Serbian and foreign), many of which have been completely unknown to public up to now". Pure advertisement, publicity, propaganda and imposition. On top of this, he was presented as a pro-European oriented politician, although he is one of the key rehabilitators of the Chetnik Movement, also the right hand of the former "civil society" of the Karađorđević dynasty.

Drašković presented his propensity for historical investigation and documentaries very well in the novel *Knife*. In it, despite historical sources, he consistently swapped the culprits for the victims. He showed himself as a forger, a falsifier, a liar, a person with sick fixations. His "documentaries" are based on a combination of lies, fiction and half-truths, as well as on "facts" at the level of "mere hearsay". *Knife* is a typical example of the literature of an author who spreads hatred and racism towards other nations. His later "literature" (*The first prayer*, *The second prayer* …) also serves to awaken and activate the lowest instincts that reached their height in the Serbian aggressions during the nineties of the last century in numerous massacres and abuse of the dead and the living. Drašković corroborated his inclination towards the study of documents also when he wrote about Stepinac on the basis of forged letters.

The renewed affirmation of Vuk Drašković in Croatia is an expression of the strength, the insolence and unscrupulousness of local Yugoslavism. *Globus* wrote that "Drašković is politically active even today… a very significant factor on the public and political scene in Serbia… he supported since 2012 – in all elections – the political option of the current President of Serbia, Aleksandar Vučić". Because this year, 2018, Chetnik Vučić was declared "European Vučić" in Croatia, it seems that *Globus* was given the task to declare Chetnik Vuk Drašković – "European Drašković". It is possible to carry out something like that only in a non-Croatian Croatia. It is therefore also feasible to expect a solemn promotion of "European Drašković's" new novel in the middle of Zagreb, partner of the "European Vučić", whose "emissary" in Croatia, a certain Pupovac, is the key factor in the "political stability" of the government of Andrej Plenković". The novel could be presented, together with Pupovac, by the Minister of Culture Nina Obuljen-Koržinek, no one would be surprised by such a scenario. Drašković too considers that – "the entire Balkan will be the strategic courtyard of the West", being aware that official Croatia has already accepted the West-Balkans positioning, which is (the anti-constitutional) prerequisite of its new Yugoslavisation in whatever form. Hence the insistence on King Aleksandar, the unifier!

The *Globus* make-over of Chetnik Vuk Drašković is the extension of the Greater Serbian aggression, the implementation of Memorandum II, the new imposition of the "soul and brain of Belgrade" and the turbo-folk marking of the century of Serbian terror in Croatia (1918 – 2018). It is the terror which was carried out with both the Yugoslav and the Greater Serbian rhetoric, with the "literature", with theory and practice. It is necessary to radically defeat both positions if Croatia wants to survive.

(hkv.hr, 25 September 2018)

The centenary celebration of the Balkan boozer in Zagreb

The celebration of the centenary (1918 - 2018) of the Belgrade Greater Serbian "annexation" of Croatia, Bosnia and Herzegovina and Vojvodina was carried out in Croatia at various levels. I have already written about the promotion of the new novel of Chetnik Vuk Drašković in the *Globus* journal. Drašković wrote a novel about the great king Karađorđević, the "unifier", who allegedly wanted to make Yugoslavia the U.S.A of the Balkans. The author, the topic of the novel and the Globus beautifully performed the celebration of the one-hundredth anniversary of the never-forgotten Yugoslavia as the extended Serbia. Unfortunately, they are not the only ones.

I did not hope that the celebration and the partying would also extend to the University of Zagreb. One month before the fatal anniversary, Rector Dr Damir Boras called for the II Rectors' Forum of the West Balkans, on 3 November. The Movement for the Croatian Future [Pokret za hrvatsku budućnost - PHB] reacted to this Yugoslav provocation on their fb page. I convey the PHB communication in full:

"The Rector of the University of Zagreb, Dr Damir Boras, called for the II Rectors' Forum of the Western Balkans, on Saturday, 3 November at 2 p.m. in the University Hall, with the participation of twenty rectors from eight countries, of which seven from countries created in the region of former Yugoslavia and Albania.

The notion of the "Western Balkans" in official and much of the non-official use in Croatia, Europe and the world, refers to the states of former

Yugoslavia, which have not yet joined the European Union. It is a matter of a technical term of the European Union, and not of a geopolitical, regional or cultural name. Since 2013, that is, from Croatia's entry into the European Union, the term is used in five, actually in six states (WB6) that are candidates or claimants to membership in the European Union: Bosnia and Herzegovina, Montenegro, Serbia, Macedonia, Kosovo and Albania (as added). It no longer refers to Slovenia and Croatia. The Croatian Government and diplomatic service have never accepted that this term is applied to the Republic of Croatia but instead preferred to speak about "Southeastern Europe". The shock is all that greater due to holding a Rectors' Forum in Zagreb according to the criterion of belonging to the "Western Balkans".

The PHB considers that the call for such congress directly defies the spirit of the Constitution of the Republic of Croatia, which in its Article 142 defines that: "It is forbidden to initiate a procedure of associating the Republic of Croatia in alliances with other states in which the association would cause, or could cause the renewal of the Yugoslav state community, or with some other Balkan state connection in whatever form". Consequently, we consider that the congress in such a format in the organization of the Rector of the University of Zagreb is an implicit geopolitical diversion. This University has just begun to celebrate the 350th anniversary of its founding in 1669. At that time, Croatia was anchored into a completely different framework – Western, central European, Mediterranean – while from the Balkans it was threatened from by unprecedented peril. In that regard, the PHB evaluates the rector's gathering within the Western-Balkans format both as a historical inversion and as a culturological obstruction of Croatian memory, belonging and identity.

It is legitimate and necessary that states and entities cooperate with others on various bases. Such as, for example, it was done and can be done within the framework of the Working Community of the Podunavlje regions, the Alps-Adriatic Working community, within that of the Mediterranean universities, the Central European initiative, the "Three seas" Initiative or the entire European Union, Europe, the United Nations and similar. However, it is not legitimate to group the leading Croatian University into the framework of the "Western Balkans" as a construct to which Croatia does not belong.

We invite all Croatian scientific and cultural institutions, as well as parties and associations which respect the Constitution of the Republic of Croatia, the heritage of the Tuđman-age and the victims of the bloody struggle for liberation from the Yugoslav "people's dungeon", and who respect the principle of sovereignty, that is, of national self-determination, to express their disagreement and bitterness, to protest and to take other steps to prevent such and possible subsequent diversions, intentionally synchronized with the 100th anniversary of the creation of the First Yugoslavia, from happening".

In this column (Erased space, hkv.hr) I announced long ago that the centenary anniversary of the Serbian occupation of Croatia, Bosnia and Herzegovina and Vojvodina will last throughout the entire year. Political Parties and cultural institutions in Croatia are watching all this in silence, pretending that nothing is happening. For the holders of the Yugoslav idea, Yugoslavia is a state that is disappearing and at the same time, it is being created in any form.

Last week we witnessed the Yugoslav extreme nationalist's posse in the context of the launch and media introduction of the Gordan Lederer Festival of Patriotic film. They are especially bothered by the dismantling of myths on which every "Yugoslavia", accompanied by brutal force and terror, was based. They are bothered by the historical truth and the reminders of a hundred years of Serbian terror over the Croats. The posse led by the local Yugo-extremes, which was not opposed by any political party, or any state or institution or high officer, was immediately exploited by Chetnik Vučić and the Serbian Minister of the Interior. As if the situation in Croatia was in the domain of Serbian interior affairs, and Croatia a "little piece" of Serbia.

As far as I know, the independent and non-clientelist veterans' scene follows with particular attention and preoccupation the neo-Yugoslav events, provocations and frauds, as well as the reflections in Croatian society and politics. Equally, bitterness is also growing towards Yugoslav extremist nationalists who have cast their web over society, the media and institutions, as well as towards the benevolent response of Croatian state institutions and Parliamentary parties in both government and the opposition.

It is good that Rector Boras unmasked himself. However, it is not good that Croatian university students and graduates, among other, are leaving both the University and the Homeland, because of Yugoslav provocations and because of the Western-Balkans positioning of the Croatian future. They are escaping as far as possible from the Balkan boozer, in which the Croatian state and Croatian people are being drowned unconstitutionally and without resistance. From a historical point of view, such actions have always provoked Croatian reactions. God forbid we wait too long!

(hkv.hr, 1 November 2018)

Analysis of documents Serbian National Council
– the future of Serbs in Croatia

The Serbian National Council does not deal at all with the Serbian national minority in Croatia, but with Serbian national rights, which can be achieved only in the Serbian national state. The achievement of Serbian national rights in Croatia is unconstitutional activity within the competence of security services. Croatia is not part of Yugoslavia in any form whatsoever. Its foundation is victory in the Homeland War, and not the late Yugoslavia (Greater Serbia).

The future of "Serbs in Croatia" or the Serbian national minority in the Republic of Croatia?

In the edition of the Serb National Council [SNV- *Srpsko narodno vijeće*], 500 copies of the Bulletin newspaper were published under the title *SNV Political Academy – the future of Serbs in Croatia*. The Bulletin was edited by Dejan Jović, prof Dr Milorad Pupovac signed as the publisher (ISSN/1849-7314). The publication was sponsored by the Office for Human Rights and Rights of National Minorities of the Government of the Republic of Croatia and the City of Zagreb. The *SNV Political Academy – the future of Serbs in Croatia* project was presented in February 2018 to the President of the Republic of Croatia and to the President of the Republic of Serbia in the presence of Metropolite Porfirije, editor Jović, the publisher Pupovac and the media.

The participants of the SNV 'Politacademy' (a total of 16) wrote answers to the questions on what they saw "as the main problems with which Serbs in Croatia are faced – at local level and on the national level". They also answered the question "how do you see the future of Serbs in Croatia in the next ten years, with the target year of 2027? What can be done – if anything can be done – so that the problems which they identified in the first question are resolved and the position of the Serbian community is improved in relation to the current situation". As can be seen in the questions, the starting point of the project is not the Serbian national minority in the Republic of Croatia, but the "Serbs in Croatia" and the "Serbian community" at local and national level.

A joint discussion followed after the homework was collected. Editor Jović wrote: "The point of the discussion and the previous essay, was to create a collective answer to the questions asked with which all, or a large majority of the participants (participants at the SNV Political Science Academy (obs.NP) can agree". The collective answer then, with which the majority agrees, is the derivative of personal opinions, feelings and discussion in a narrow circle of participants and "activists from the ranks of the Serbian community". The objectivity of the collective answer, however, is a question that needs an answer. The document consists of two parts. Here we are dealing with the first part.

A century of Serbian terror 1918 - 2018

Regarding the problems on the local level, the participants of Jović's academy and the activists of Pupovac's SNV, adopted several "collective answers" on which the majority agreed. Firstly, there is the poor "local infrastructure, especially in villages where Serbs form the majority of inhabitants". The problem might be real, however, nobody in Croatia has a poor communal infrastructure just because they are a member of Serbian or any other national minority. A problem defined in this way constitutes perfidious deceit. The state would be facing total disintegration if every national minority claimed that it has poor local infrastructure just because it belongs to a certain minority. In general, a serious national minority behaves seriously at local and national level. However, the SNV is not a national minority; self-proclaimed and unsupervised by the government yet heavily financed by the state, it prepares "collective answers", that is, renews the runways of political Serbianism in Croatia.

In second place is the problem of "the lack of cultural content in small places, especially in villages". Therefore, a "feeling is created" that "all the activities are carried out in bigger cities". The collective answer of the SNV Political Academy concludes that the mentioned "feeling" – "creates the need for migration from small places and gives rise to a feeling of neglect". Here we have the synergy of two unpleasant feelings. Both of them, apparently, can be solved with stronger involvement of the SNV cultural component and the reduction of the SNV political component, which includes demands like the introduction of the Cyrillic alphabet in Vukovar, of the Serbian language in the Croatian Parliament, territorial ghettos like the SAO and RSK, or demands for the status of *politički narod* [a political nation] in Croatia.

The third collective answer as formulated by the participants and the SNV activists is the "lack of coordination of politics at national level with those at local level". That is, "although Serbian representatives are involved in politics at the national level, they are not everywhere at the local level", and if they are involved, there is insufficient coordination between the representatives at those two levels". The problem is how to create the conditions that "Serbian representatives" are represented "everywhere at a local level". This recipe is known from history. Namely, so that all Serbs live in one state. The solution can be achieved in Serbia and the Serbian Republic headed by the European Vučić and Dodik.

Another of the local problems: "In the regions where the war has left more visible trace, there is a greater distance between Serbs and Croats. In other areas the problems of assimilation and 'hiding of identity' are more distinctive". In the Bulletin, the "war" is not defined as the Greater Serbian aggression with the plebiscitary rebellion of "Serbs in Croatia" and the "Serbian community". It is simply a war. The assimilation of national minorities is noticeable in all states. For example, the assimilation of the Croatian national minority in Serbia is unforeseeable today, while compulsory emigration of minority Croats from Serbia was an integral part of the Greater Serbian aggression.

The serious issues with collective problems mentioned in the Bulletin, start with the list of common ones at local and national level. The participants and SNV activists included in the first place the "negative description of Serbs in the media, including also the most important media". The document does not mention any example of media in Croatia that has negatively portrayed Croats who are members of the Serbian national minority. The collective answer, however, states – "due to the negative role of the media it remains 'uncomfortable to be a Serb or a Serbian woman'". With this, the conclusion in the Bulletin introduces also the third feeling (the discomfort). There are now three bad feelings: the lacking, the neglect and the discomfort. In synergy, they lead towards the cult of endangering Croats of Serbian nationality.

Following the introduction of the cult of endangering based on emotions, there comes the main, great lie in the best tradition of Greater Serbian ideology. The collective SNV answer mentions as the second problem inherent in local and national levels, "the trend of 'new fascistisation' in the society which is visible also with the increase in the number of attacks on Serbs and on objects/symbols that are significant to the Serbian national identity". In Croatia, the Croats of Serbian nationality can only have minority identity and not a national one. Furthermore, Croatia remains, according to the Serbs, always to a certain degree fascist, ever since "the sixteenth century" (V. Krestić). Not a single exact indicator is mentioned about the increase in the "number of attacks", or that it is the undoubted consequence of the "new fascistisation in society". The Bulletin therefore calls on previous SNV Bulletins and states that: "Since 2013, as the reports published in the

SNV Bulletins indicate, the number of physical attacks is increasing, which encourages anxiety and fear as well as the desire to 'hide one's identity', namely for ethnic mimicry".

The next local national problems are "assimilation trends, which are visible in a *podozrenje* towards the use of words belonging specifically to the Serbian variant of the language, as well as in the hesitation to celebrate Serbian holidays, especially the baptismal celebration" (Serb *podozrenje* = doubt, suspicion, distrust).

The consistent implementation of Article 12 of the Constitution of the Republic of Croatia is not assimilation – in Croatia the official language is the Croatian language. However, guessing about an alleged existence of a Serbian version of the Croatian language is justified. The Serbian version of the Croatian language does not exist constitutionally or legally. Serbian holidays in the Republic of Croatia are not Croatian holidays. All holidays are regulated by the law and refer to all citizens of the Republic of Croatia. Some of them are not accepted by the "Serbs in Croatia" and the "Serbian community" (Victory Day and Homeland Thanksgiving, Croatian Veterans Day, Remembrance Day of 1991 Vukovar victims…). They celebrate some of the non-existent holidays (in the town of Srb, Rebellion Day of the Croatian People) – that is an objective problem. Baptismal celebrations are family holidays for Orthodox believers. The believers in the Croatian Orthodox Church do not express any problems in that regard. Therefore, it can be deduced that this "problem" actually does not exist.

A new local national problem refers to the "departure of young Serbs from Croatia, especially from the areas where there are no employment possibilities". Emigration is a common problem in Croatia and it is not related specifically to the Serbian national minority. Naturally, "it leads to a very bad age structure in the population". However, "it is noted that the Serbian inhabitants, on average, are much older than the Croatian population". So? Why the age comparison of the Serbian national minority with the age structure of the *politički narod* [the home nation] in the national state of the Croatian nation? The comparison indicates the intention toward the Yugo-communist-Greater Serbian model of the subjugated Croatia with two political nations, where the less numerous one had to be privileged in everything and that is where the "age structure" comparison comes from. Political nations are compared with political nations, national minorities with national minorities.

Then it's the turn of material rights with the emphasis on "refugees". "Discrimination in the implementation of rights that are guaranteed by law, and especially in employment and obtaining services of social welfare and health care, of former tenants' rights and pension rights. This refers especially to persons who were refugees, and who faced many difficulties in the achievement of their rights upon their return to Croatia". This is no longer a matter of feelings, but of direct claims. Are they true?

The Serbian national minority in Croatia enjoys incredible rights. It is not discriminated. On the contrary. And if it looks like it is discriminated, then it is less discriminated than the Croatian political people regarding the returnees. Namely, upon their return to Croatia from the diaspora, although they are the members of the political national majority, the Croats achieved fewer rights than the returnees of Serbian national minority who participated in the aggression on Croatia and who later left voluntarily because they did not accept the Republic of Croatia as their Homeland, and despite not being the political national majority. The Bulletin sees no problem with that. Therefore, even that alleged discrimination is not a specific problem for the Serbian national minority in Croatia. But it is an expression of the aspiration to become a *politički narod* in the national state of the Croatian people, who are the only *politički narod* in the Republic of Croatia. The one that finances the SNV and its political and media projects.

Legal uncertainty is also included in Serbian problems at local and national level. The "members of the Serbian community feel this in relation to the judiciary". It is again a matter of the combination of "Serbian community" and "the feelings", instead of the Serbian national minority and objective indicators. In other words, the "Serbs do not feel that sentencing is neutral in relation to national affiliation". The Croats however, can prove exactly, not according to feelings, that because of their national affiliation and readiness to defend the Homeland from the Greater Serbian aggression, they are treated by the Croatian (non-lustrated) judiciary according to the criterion of equalising the aggressor and the victim.

Also problematic are the "trials in absence and arrests at borders of Serbs who live abroad …, and the judges do not judge everyone equally". Those Croats of Serbian nationality who live abroad, are not members of the Serbian national minority in Croatia, however, it appears that they are part of the "Serbian community" and the "Serbs in Croatia". There is not a single word mentioned in this document on whether the Croats, of any nationality, are disturbed by the fact that the criminals of Serb nationality from the era of the Greater Serbian aggression are not being prosecuted, which should be important for the future of the Serbian national minority. The SNV document cannot possibly consider that "Serbs in Croatia" and "the Serbian community" include, as equal members of the Serbian national minority, the non-convicted Chetniks, terrorists, cut-throats, rapists, war criminals, ministers of the occupiers' fabrication of the Republic of Serbian Krajina, presidents and assembly members of the outlaw "councils of municipalities", regions and border-lands. If they do belong there, then the entire Serbian national minority is right about the legal uncertainty, because some crimes do not become obsolete. That is why they must be individualized, one by one, found, arrested, transferred and rightly judged. The document is remarkably silent about whether the Serbian so-called universal law is problematic, though it directly or indirectly damages the Serbian national minority in Croatia.

The next problem of the Political Science Academy and its 16 participants is the following – "the unfulfilled promises – at all levels". Oh, we can partially agree on that, because, as we can see, "Many things are promised to Serbs before the elections" also. However, the majority of people cannot agree with the rest – "as a rule after the elections, nothing of what was offered materializes". Namely, neither in Sanader time, nor in Plenković time, did they promise before the election that the HDZ party would enter the ruling coalition with the SDSS Serbian party. After the election, through the HDZ electoral fraud, the SDSS became part of the Government. After the elections, therefore, the "Serbian community" obtained even more political and *sine cura* job rights than it was promised before the elections. The issue of post-election frauds is a stick with two ends, but again, it is not related specifically to the Serbian national minority, to which it actually refers least. With the post-election fraud, the political majority are the ones who lose the most, yet that, of course, is not presented as a problem in the document. The problem mentioned is, in fact, not at all a problem of the Serbian national minority. It is a problem of the SNV unappeasable appetite, its president, who is on a direct line with Belgrade of which President Vučić recently personally testified to the "Serbs in Croatia" in the Lisinski Hall and the "Serb community" in the areas liberated by Operation Storm.

There are more problems. Let's emphasize: "the poverty of the Serbian inhabitants". That is a general Croatian problem. Nobody in Croatia is poor because he is a Croat of Serbian national minority.

Notes for further deliberation on the future of the SNC community and Serbian national minority:

1. The Bulletin of the *SNV Political Sciences Academy – the future of Serbs in Croatia* in its first part, while describing the work methodology and providing collective answers and quoting the most important problems, did not once use the constitutionally correct term "Serbian national minority in Croatia". Instead, it uses the legally non-existent terms "Serbian community" and "Serbs in Croatia". Therefore, the Bulletin is the source of the problem, and not a solution.

2. The goal of the project was to reach a "collective answer" of the entire "Serbian community" and the "Serbs in Croatia" on the basis of the work and discussion of the "16 participants" of Dejan Jović's SNV Political Sciences Academy. Consequently, it follows that the document published in the SNV Bulletin, supported by the Zagreb Government, does not refer at all to the Serbian national minority in Croatia, nor can it objectively express its "collective" opinion about the future until 2017. Despite that, it was presented as relevant to the presidents of the two states of the "territory of former Yugoslavia", and as far as the public is aware, to no one else.

3. The publisher: "the SNV deals with the protection and promotion of human, civil and national rights of Serbs, as well as with the issues of their identity, participation and integration into the Croatian society. The Council was established on the basis of the Erdut Agreement". The Erdut Agreement did not foresee the establishment of the SNV. The Erdut Agreement refers to the "transitional period" which expired a long time ago. Therefore, the SNV does not deal at all with the Serb national minority in Croatia, but with Serb national rights, which can be achieved

A century of Serbian terror 1918 - 2018

only in the national state of the Serbs. The achievement of national rights of Serbs in Croatia is an unconstitutional activity under the competence of security services.

4. The publisher who signed is the SNV president Milorad Pupovac, who is also the President of the SDSS Party, which involves a civil society association and a political party in a conflict of interest. The Commission for Conflict of Interests avoids to discuss this issue. A further objective problem is that the SDSS is the political "party which unites, shapes and directs the political will and actions of the Serbian community in the Republic of Croatia", and not of the Serbian national minority. A community or a national minority, a question which, in view of the future requires a clear answer by the majority people and before that, a decision as to what the so-called national minority actually is in Croatia. The signed publisher skillfully manipulates between the different concepts and designations, and on the basis of manipulation achieves political and personal goals and advantages. Perhaps also fallacies.

5. The editor of the Bulletin (No. 13) and head of the SNV Academy is a professor at the Faculty of Political Sciences. In view of the Bulletin's unfounded direct accusations of Croatia for discrimination, fascism, assimilation, legal insecurity, infrastructural neglect, linguistic ridicule and media satanisation of the "Serbs in Croatia" and the "Serbian community" at local and national levels of the Croatian national state, the question arises regarding what does prof Dejan Jović teach Croatian university students, if he represents and edits the cult and myth of the endangered Serb in Croatia and creates the artificial fascistisation of the Croatian state within the civil society.

6. The SNV Bulletin uses an empty (scientific, objective) space and fills it with subjective feelings and chewed up myths, instead of encouraging objective, independent scientific investigations about the position and projection of the future for the Serbian national minority in Croatia.

7. The document divides the Serbian national minority in Croatia into local and national, pretending that precisely the SNV represents the "Serbian community". The purpose of the division is to prove the endangering of the "Serbian community" and the "Serbs in Croatia", wherever in Croatia they live, work, or are emigrating, or immigrating as "refugees". The endangering is omnipresent also in relation to the total, local and national, territorial and administrative corpus of the Croatian state, and it is the basis for the modernization of the cult and refreshing of the myth of the endangered Serb.

8. The main structure of the mentioned problems accuses Croatia of a) media satanisation, b) new fascistising, c) language inequality and d) legal uncertainty. With that, the document actually demands even more pronounced media privilege, anti-fascist privilege, language unitarism and legal immunity for the "Serbs in Croatia" and the "Serbian community".

8.a) The SNV publishes annual journals in which it satanises Croats. The SNV publishes the weekly Novosti newspaper, in which the values inherited by the national political majority are continually derided. With this, both media create serious problems and division in the relations between the national majority and the loyal Serbian national minority. The document does not say a single word about this objective problem. The Bulletin, therefore, uses the method of switching theses, since it is the SNV media who satanise and label their victims in the media.

8.b) The new fascistisation is a dangerous fabrication of non-lustrated communists and Greater Serbs, who carry out their common politics under the aegis of "anti-fascism". The fascistisation, however, actually does exist in as much as it is artificially [*veštački* in Serbian] produced. It is produced, among other, also in the SNV. The document does not see the production of the fascistisation as an objective problem for the future of the "Serbs in Croatia", yet it is undoubtedly a problem for the Serbian national minority in Croatia, as well as the political national majority and their national state.

8.c) The problems [in the Bulletin] do not highlight the practice of SDSS representatives (the case of the representative Dragana Jeckov) speaking in Serbian language in the Croatian Parliament, by which the Rules of Procedure of the Croatian Parliament and the Constitution of the Republic of Croatia are violated and additional acceleration is added towards the "common language", that is, the unitarst language. The Political Sciences Academy document does not see the disrespect for Croatian, as the official language, by the "Serbs in Croatia" and the

"Serbian community", as a problem that affects their future until 2027. What is worse, it is probably right for as long as electoral fraud rules in Croatia, which directly benefits the Publisher and the person who signed "for the Publisher".

8.d) Is it a problem affecting the future of the "Serbs in Croatia" that from time to time, the Croatian judiciary condemns a member of the "Serbian community" who participated in the aggression on the Republic of Croatia and committed a crime that does not become obsolete? If it is, does that mean that the SNV Political Sciences Academy and the SNV are advocating a universal jurisdiction of Serbian judiciary? Is it, then, not a feeling, but an objective problem for the Croatian state? Why does the SNV Political Sciences Academy keep silent about this and does not treat it as a problem that needs to be resolved?

9. The document consistently avoids historical contexts and its attitude toward the aggression on Croatia (by Serbia, Montenegro and the rebel Serbs in Croatia). None of the problems mentioned in the document was a problem at the time of the Socialist Republic of Croatia and the Republic of Serbian Krajina, in which Serbs were a *politički narod* with the right to secession or with a materialized/consummated right to secession.

10. Most parts of the document appeal to "feelings". Nowhere does it call on exact data. In one part it calls on previous internal interpretations of the SNV Publisher. The document does not accept any information outside the SNV circle. Thus, in a way it is single-minded, although it should be informationally pluralistic when it speaks about such a serious topic as the future until 2027.

11. For the future of the Serbian national minority in Croatia, it is extremely important to respect the Constitution of the Republic of Croatia. The disrespect of the Constitution, however, is not pointed out as a local problem, or as a national problem, although it is a basic problem.

12. The document is dominantly written from the platform of qualifications which are valid only within the SNV. Therefore, the document cannot contribute to reconciliation, integration and coexistence. The results available from scientific institutions are excluded *a priori,* and, for example, the warnings of security services of the Republic of

Croatia about the rise in leftist and Chetnik extremism, which definitely affect the future of "Serbs in Croatia", but even more the future of the Serbian national minority in Croatia.

13. None of the claims of which the authors of the document accuse the Republic of Croatia for its allegedly discriminatory position have been corroborated with objective data (in numbers: 0).

14. In the part where the document accuses the Republic of Croatia of (at least) the "new fascistisation", the document is actionable in the line of duty and it should be transferred to the focus and competence of the State Attorney. Especially because it is presented to the highest levels of government of the two states, Croatia and Serbia, whom the document might have led to fallacy and by which the document achieves also an international dimension (at the level of, in truth, a non-existent Western Balkans), but which as such could have influence on the Western Balkans strategy of the European Union, which would be very detrimental to the newly fascistised Croatia.

15. From recent historical experience we can conclude that, unlike the loyal Serbian national minority, the "Serbs in Croatia" and the SNVs "Serbian community" did not have problems with feelings, new fascistisation, judiciary, number of attacks, language and municipal infrastructure in the occupied areas of the internationally acknowledged territory of the Republic of Croatia.

15.1 The first part of the Bulletin does not mention problems that might have arisen from the uprising of the Serbs in Croatia aligned with the Serbian and Montenegrin aggression on Croatia, nor does it say anything about whether the consequences of the internal fifth colony rebellions have reflections on today's situation in which there are insufficient cultural events and quality infrastructure, but there are different feelings.

15.2 In the 2027 projection, the Bulletin does not say to which extent the mentioned problems of the "Serbs in Croatia" and the "Serbian community" could be solved by the payment of war compensation for the destroyed municipal, cultural, sacral, health, educational, traffic and all other infrastructure caused in the "war" on the territory of the Republic of Croatia, by the aggressors: Serbia, Montenegro and the rebel "Serbs in Croatia".

How to improve the situation of the non-existent political people in Croatia?

As introduction to the second part of Bulletin 13, *The SNV Political Sciences Academy – the future of Serbs in Croatia,* the editor stated "the five main problems faced by the current generation of Serbian women and men in Croatia". The participants at the Academy and SNV activists highlighted the "economic underdevelopment" in the "areas where Serbs are more numerous" as the biggest problem. The economic underdevelopment in Croatia is not related to any national minority, or the Serbian national minority.

Then it's the turn of the problems "with the issues of identity and creation of public perception". They are a "direct consequence of the lengthening and constant emphasizing of the war as basis of the Croatian identity and the continuous creation of feelings of collective guilt that involve the entire Serb population in Croatia". The direct consequence of the "war" (that is – the Greater Serbian aggression), among other things, is also Croatia's economic lagging behind. The issue of Serbian identity and its perception in the Croatian state is not tied up with the imposition of collective guilt on the Serbian national minority. The problem is that the "Serbs in Croatia" impose the collective guilt on the national majority and their national state, while they do not acknowledge that the liberation Homeland War is the basis of the Republic of Croatia. Between 1945 and today, several generations of the national majority are included in that collective guilt, while the elite of "Serbs in Croatia" made an excellent living from the production of that guilt. The imposition of collective guilt on Croats and on the Croatian state is one of the important causes of the emigration of Croats and of the "economic underdevelopment" of their national state.

The next problem is the "inequality and impossibility to achieve rights, even those guaranteed by the Constitution and the laws". In relation to the Croats, the "Serbs in Croatia" are more equal, because they enjoy the "positive discrimination", which was given to them, despite the will of the majority people, by the denationalised elites and the deep state composed of non-lustrated remnants of the communist totalitarian regime. The rights in Croatia are achieved at the same pace by all citizens regardless of their national affiliation, unless they are from the Croatian emigration or Bosnia and Herzegovina - they either cannot achieve them at all, or achieve them with big obstacles from the deep state to which the non-lustrated elites of the "Serbs from Croatia" also belong. As far as the rights are concerned, they are inseparable from duty. The right question is to what extent does the disruption and denial of Church and public holidays prescribed by law, as well as the commemorations of Croatian victims killed by the totalitarian regimes of monarchist and communist Yugoslavia, the terrorist-totalitarian regime of the Republic of Serbian Krajina and of the Chetnik rebellions against Croatian statehood, contribute to the problems.

The problems include "education and training that could enable active economic and social life". The "unfavourable demographic trends", caused by "strong assimilation trends, the age structure of the inhabitants and a more intensive departure of young Serbian women and men from Croatia" are also a problem. If the "Serbs from Croatia" are leaving Croatia due to assimilation, then how to explain the departure of young Croatian women and men, Italian women and men, Czech women and men… Is it due to assimilation? The Republic of Croatia does not have exact data on the latest wave of emigration. Thus, at this moment there are no data that corroborate the "more intensive departure of young Serbian women and Serbian men from Croatia".

The next part of Bulletin 13 refers to the problems of the "Serbian community". The notion of "Serbian community" is not defined there. It is assumed, implied (it has already been adopted somewhere), it can be widely interpreted, depending on personal feelings and collective perceptions. The Serbian community might mean a community of all Serbs in the world, Serbs in Serbia, Serbs of the Western Balkans, Serbs gathered around the SNV, Serbs in the Greater Serbia, Serbs "disseminated" gathered around the RSK Government in "exile", and so on. The Republic of Croatia does not know that term. Croatia speaks about the Serbian national minority.

The "Serbian community" observed the "lack of a clear strategy in their own development", and that "it was demonstrated that the 'great coalition' model is beneficial to the Serbian community, so it is necessary to reach broader legitimacy and unity on strategic questions". The reference is obviously one to the need for political strategy in the interests of political Serbianism in Croatia, and not the strategy of the development of the Serbian national minority in the Republic of Croatia. Where to start writing the "strategy"? From "Serbs all and everywhere", from *Načertanije*, from *Homogeneous Serbia*, from the "SANU Memorandum", or from the Constitution of the Republic of Croatia? A strategy is not a strategy without determining the "formative sources". Who is going to pay for the writing of the strategy? The Government office and the City of Zagreb?

The "Serbian community" also has "heterogeneity issues regarding its identity", which is a consequence of its "dissemination within Croatia", so it is necessary to work on the internal familiarising and exchange of "experiences that are not the same in all parts of Croatia". The issue of the heterogeneity could be solved with homogenising the "Serbian community". However, even when the "Serbian community" was homogenised in the RSK, it did not solve any problem, but created many new ones. It seems that in order to solve not only this problem, it would be best that the "Serbian community" accepts the status of national minority in the Republic of Croatia and starts dealing with issues with which all national minorities in the European Union are dealing.

Furthermore, "it is necessary to break within the community the taboo topics that refer to the past and to stay open for dialogue with others, first of all with Croats, with whom we live in almost all the places of Croatia". The "Serbian community" lives with Croats in all parts of Croatia, regardless of their national affiliation. The members of the "Serbian community" are also Croats, if they live in the national state of the Croatian nation.

Furthermore, "the community should not split into ghettos, and its relationship with other communities, and especially the Croatian community, must be based on principles of citizens' solidarity, and not on the politics of 'we' and 'they'". There is no such thing as a Croatian community in the Republic of Croatia, only the Croatian people. The "Serbian community" became a ghetto the moment it accepted the combination of extensible terms "Serbian community" and "Serbs in Croatia", instead of the constitutional term, which defines it within the Republic of Croatia.

The Republic of Croatia is not a state of different communities. It is a national state of Croatian people. A citizen of the Republic of Croatia is called a Croat. Such as French in France. Should the "taboo be broken" within the "Serbian community" regarding topics which refer to the past, the majority people will accept a dialogue. Where should the dialogue start from? From breaking the taboo of the Chetnik uprising in the town of Srb? From Operation Storm? From the causes of the Greater Serbian aggression? Who will lead that dialogue on behalf of the "Serbian community"? The editor Jović or the publisher Pupovac, the minister of the terrorist government of the RSK Stanimirović or the "European" Vučić of Glina, the ideologists of the "Serbian community" or the ethno-businessmen of "Serbs in Croatia"?

The fascination with the Croats is evident in the following problem, which states that it is necessary "to work more on ourselves so that the Serbs in Croatia are successful" (not anymore the "Serbian community", obs. NP) and "become the model not only to the Serbs in Croatia, but also to the Croats. That would best change the image of the Serbs". In the Republic of Croatia, the Serbs can be a model to Croats only if Serbian eminence is forcefully imposed on the Croats! And in no other way. Nowhere in the world does a national minority work on themselves so that they become a model to the majority political people. Does the "change of the Serb image" represent a breakthrough from national minority into a political nation? The point in this article is defined unambiguously and it can be interpreted, and read, as renewal of relations already seen in force when the Serbs were a political nation in Croatia, which ended in Croatia with the abolition of the Yugo-communist system, the introduction of the democratic system and the renewal of the Croatian national state, and its liberation from the Greater Serbian occupation.

Fifth, "it is necessary to introduce into the public life more firmly a new generation of Serbian women and men, those born after 1991" who "did not participate in war events", because "they would have more possibility to gain Croatian confidence and organize a new agenda, oriented toward the future. That new generation should try to get out of traditionalist frames that are inadequate for the new age". It is good to think of new generations. However, it is not the SNVs task to introduce into the public, that is, political life, Serbs and Serbian women born

A century of Serbian terror 1918 - 2018

anytime and anywhere. It is best for the members of the Serbian national minority to enter the public, political life through legal institutions and parties, and not through structures of "Serbian community" ideologists and "Serbs in Croatia" ethno-businessmen.

Furthermore, the document recommends tactics for political Serbs on how "it is necessary to use the power of the veto more meaningfully and more appropriately in order to achieve goals that are important for the Serbian community". The veto of a national minority, in every national state and beyond is no small joke anymore, just as is to "draw a bottom line under which political options that do not respect the interests of Serbian voters will not be supported".

This means that should it be in the interest of Serbian voters, who are in fact part of the List of Voters in the Republic of Croatia, that the town of Srb is declared the anti-fascist uprising of people, or that Operation Storm is a criminal undertaking of a genocidal nation, and the government disagrees with that, then Pupovac will hand in the veto. Political radicalization is not in the interest of the Serbian national minority in the Republic of Croatia. Where there are national minorities in the states of the European Union, they generally incline toward the political option that wins the majority in the elections without their votes. That is elementary and decent behavior. The veto is the expression of a *politički narod*. The Serbs are not (yet) that political entity in the Republic of Croatia, although it seems (repeatedly) that they are.

Finally, we arrive to the solutions and the answers to the question "what should be done to improve the situation in the next ten years?".

First. The "Serbian community must work on self-sustainability, wherever that is possible!" What is self-sustainability? Let us assume for a moment, that self-sustainability is not related to autocracy (a form of imperial government in former imperial Russia, related to absolutism), but let us not forget that notion either. How can a "community" achieve self-sustainability when we know that Serbia is not an Amish community, and that the Republic of Croatia is not the U.S.A.? No way. The "Serbian community" cannot realistically be self-sustainable in the territorial, transport, economic, energetic, educational, administrative, security or every other regard. True, the "Serbian community" achieved the highest degree of self-sustainability, unconstitutionally, in the Republic of Serbian Krajina. And it proved to be self-unsustainable. The self-sustainability of the "Serbian community" in Croatia is possible only in the fantasies about Greater Serbia in which the "Serbian community" in Croatia would become a "small piece" of the "complete Serbian people" who live in one state. Such a Greater Serbia cannot survive if it includes one inch of Croatian internationally acknowledged territory. Self-sustainability is unconstitutional.

It is surprising that the participants and activists were not warned about that by professors Jović and Pupovac, who have direct experience in the fall of Serbian self-sustainability utopia in the Republic of Croatia. Why do they lead a new generation of "Serbian women and men" into old fallacies? Because of the "dialogue with Croats", because of "gaining the Croats confidence", the "change in the image about the Serbs"? Nevertheless, the document highlights in the first place the encouragement of "private and group entrepreneurial initiative and leaning more about themselves than it was the case up to now". Much as it leans on private and group enterprise, the "Serbian community cannot reach economic self-sustainability in the Republic of Croatia if it does not have the monetary power, payment system, territory, army, police, customs, borders and other elements of full statehood. Self-sustainability does not exist without full statehood. The states which can survive self-sustainably in the "global village" are a rarity. No national minority in any European Union country has achieved self-sustainability. Surely, here we are not thinking about the self-sustainability in the financing of the mentioned community without the participation of the state budget of the Republic of Croatia.

Second. Political representatives, this time of the "Serbs in Croatia", must "secure that the state, counties and municipalities do not create obstacles to such an initiative (towards the self-sustainability of "Serbian community", obs. NP). They should enable it, instead, primarily with the creation of conditions: legal, practical, and especially infrastructural, which are the basis for small and medium enterprise, education and the development of Serb culture and identity in Croatia. It was proposed to secure special development funds and intensify the work of the Centre for Development and Investment". Before defining more precisely the notion of self-sustainability of the "Serbian community" with the help of the representatives of "Serbs in Croatia", the state, county and municipality, certain previous notions must be defined, in order to know at least who, what and where is seeking self-sustainability, and what are the goals of self-sustainability of the "Serbs in Croatia" within the Croatian national state.

Third. The "collaboration (here again of "Serbs in Croatia", obs. NP) with Croats based on common interests is useful for all and it must be encouraged". What common interests can the majority people and the Serbs in Croatia have? The self-sustainability of the "Serbian community"? Again, the focus is transferred to the political field instead of to the minority. That is, "up to now, the inclusion of Serb representatives in institutions was frequently only a formality, but in reality, they still remained excluded from the real process of decision making or were faced with insurmountable obstacles". Are the functions within the national state such as – state secretary, minister assistant, minister – a formality, exclusion and insurmountable obstacle to the "Serbs in Croatia"?

Fourth. "It is necessary to continue developing Serb institutions and organizations in Croatia, which must be inclusive and based on principles of solidarity and understanding". The influence of Plenković's 'centralistic' rhetoric on the "Serbian community's" vocabulary is obvious, which makes it possible that also his politics is included in the document, given that publisher Pupovac characterized the current head of Government as "pure gold". However, the inclusivism is here understood unilaterally – only as the inclusion of the minority into the majority. Bilateral inclusion is lacking: that of the majority that forms the national state into the minority. The values of the majority are entirely excluded.

Fifth. Among the solutions that can improve the alarming situation described in the first part of the document, there is also the instruction – "the benefits of the membership in the European Union must be used in order to faster develop the undeveloped areas. Many of them are exactly the ones where the Serbs in Croatia live". Not only the benefits of the membership in the European Union, but there should also be the "increase in the coordination of those issues, perhaps through a special and permanent economic forum which would link the Serbian diaspora with local entrepreneurs, and through the creation of an enterprise register".

What is meant here by "Serbian diaspora"? "Serbs in Croatia" who left Croatia? Why does the Republic of Croatia need a register of Serbian entrepreneurs, is this not an argument to group the Serbian national minority into ghettos? What Croatia needs is a register of Serbs from Croatia who rebelled against the constitutional system. That is the path towards the solution of the problem, not registers made according to a national basis. Does the SNV Political Science Academy want to "count the blood cells" of Croatian entrepreneurs?

Sixth. The need is highlighted for "an active approach" toward the "categories which, due to their importance for Serbian inhabitants, require special care: for example, the youth, demographic politics, the issue of the return or inclusion of those who had left into development issues, and the elderly who today represent an important part of the Serbian community in Croatia".

"Serbian inhabitants" is a new conception. Serbian inhabitants live in Serbia. Italian inhabitants live in Italy. Croatian inhabitants live in Croatia. "Serbian inhabitants" in Croatia can be deciphered only as inhabitants of the political nation. It is symptomatic that the document acknowledges that also those "who left" represent "an important part of Serbian community in Croatia". In other words, if a member of the Serbian national minority left Croatia, they are no longer a member of the Serbian national minority in Croatia. Therefore, they cannot represent an "important part of Serbian community in Croatia". They are not diaspora either, because national minorities do not have diaspora, only a political people have diaspora.

The third part of the document gives abstracts on the essays with answers, and we do not refer to that here, that is, the sample is too small to allow conclusions being drawn on it. We therefore only deal with the "collective answers" and recommendations.

The second part of the stated document considers the fundamental question to be: how to change the status of the unrecognised into a recognised political nation in the Republic of Croatia? The solutions offered can be sublimated as follows:

1. By non-acceptance of the constitutional term "Serbian national minority".

A century of Serbian terror 1918 - 2018

2. By manipulating the notions "Serbian community", "Serbs in Croatia", "Serbian inhabitants".

3. By insisting on "wherever possible" on the self-sustainability of the "Serbian community".

4. By demanding that the political representatives of "Serbs in Croatia" ensure the self-sustainability of the "Serbian community" so that "obstacles are not created" towards it, but to enable it with the creation of legal conditions.

5. By cooperating with Croats on the basis of common interests, so that the "Serbian community", although still wholly unsustainable, is placed in the constitutional position with the political majority people.

6. By continuing to develop institutions and organisations of "Serbs in Croatia".

7. By strengthening the business and economic basis and "through a special and sustained economic forum, which would connect the Serbian diaspora (from Croatia) with local entrepreneurs (Serbs in Croatia), as well as through the creation of a register of (Serbian) entrepreneurs (in Croatia)".

8. By strengthening targeted groups of "Serbian inhabitants" (in Croatia), namely: a) the youth, b) returnees (from "diaspora"), c) "those who left" (from the Serbian community in Croatia to diaspora), and d) elderly inhabitants – they are all "an important part of the Serbian community in Croatia", because the program of converting the unpolitical people into a political people [*politički narod*] can be achieved only with the increase of "Serbian inhabitants" within the Croatian people.

Is it an exaggeration to conclude that "Serbs in Croatia" are trying to become a political nation? Stanimirović has recently introduced the Serbian SDSS Party into the pre-electoral coalition of the SDP Party ("Croatia is growing") with the aim to obtain one mandate on the coalition list in Vukovar, beside the three mandates that are already guaranteed. He said: "By obtaining this mandate, together with the three in the 12th minority unit, Serbs in Croatia also become a *politički narod*, not only a minority".

From the sublimated solutions, which would allegedly improve the allegedly poor situation of the target "community", which also introduces itself as "people" in Croatia, it can be concluded that the "Serbian community", "Serbs in Croatia", "Serbian inhabitants" and "Serbian diaspora" from Croatia:

1. Despise the status of the Serbian national minority in Croatia.

2. Are trying to achieve the status of a political nation in Croatia.

3. Are trying to convince the Serbian national minority that it is possible to be a self-sustaining community in Croatia.

4. Give legitimacy to their political representatives, ideologists and ethno-businessmen to demand from the state the creation of legal conditions for self-sustainability of the "Serbian community".

5. Ask to find Croats with whom they share a "common interest", so that with their help they can carry out single nation self-sustainability.

6. Offer development of the organisation of Serbs in Croatia, instead of the Serbian national minority.

7. Are introducing the notion of their own "diaspora" in order to achieve the position of a political nation indirectly since a direct method is not feasible due to the low number of "Serbs in Croatia".

8. Are introducing the notion of "Serbian inhabitants" in the Republic of Croatia.

Bulletin 13 is in its essence a political program of a group of Croats, Croatian citizens, of Serbian nationality from Croatia, gathered around the single-nation civil society association paid by the Croatian national and local budget. The program tries to substitute the Yugo-communist designation of Croatia as Homeland to two political peoples. It is an expression of the anti-democratic, Yugoslav and communist aspiration that a minority dictates the conditions to the majority.

To what extent is this aspiration in accord with the Constitution of the Republic of Croatia, and how much with the goals of the Republic of Serbia in Croatia, is a theme for serious interdisciplinary scientific analysis and represents a challenge to political parties, the constitutional and legal system and the relevant services within the Republic of Croatia.

(hkv.hr, 13 and 20 March 2018)

A century of Serbian terror 1918 - 2018

About the author

With this book, Nenad Piskač (Zagreb, 8 August 1962) has published seventeen books to date in the areas of literature, political and historical publicism. He has published systematically since 1986.

He writes literary work (poetry, travel books, short essays, movie scenarios, and literature for children) in standard Croatian language and in kajkavian dialect. His work is included in several anthology selections of poetry and travel books. Two feature-length documentaries were filmed to his scenarios.

Piskač worked in different publishing firms, some established by himself, as journalist, editor and editor-in-chief. He edited numerous literary editions and anthologies (The days of Dr Franjo Tuđman – Croats through centuries; The Kajkavian in the current and future settings). He is a pensioner with disability since 2013.

He writes in Vukovo Selo. He is married and has four children. He is a Homeland War veteran, a National Guard Assembly volunteer and Croatian defender in the operative section of the Croatian Army (with Homeland War commemorative medal, and the Flash and Storm operations medals). He is a member of the Association of Croatian Writers.

Piskač is a long-time columnist of the Croatian Cultural Council portal (hkv.hr) and member of the prize-awarding Artistic Committee of the Gordan Lederer Patriot Film Festival. (ed.)

www.ingramcontent.com/pod-product-compliance
Lightning Source LLC
Chambersburg PA
CBHW061759250726
48657CB00001B/203